ECONOMIC ANALYSIS OF INSTITUTIONS AND SYSTEMS
Revised Second Edition

International Studies in Economics and Econometrics

VOLUME 33

The titles published in this series are listed at the end of this volume.

Economic Analysis of Institutions and Systems

Revised Second Edition

Svetozar Pejovich
*Department of Economics,
Texas A&M University,
College Station, Texas*

KLUWER ACADEMIC PUBLISHERS
Dordrecht / Boston / London

Distributors for North America:
Kluwer Academic Publishers
101 Philip Drive
Assinippi Park
Norwell, Massachusetts 02061 USA

Distributors for all other countries:
Kluwer Academic Publishers Group
Distribution Centre
Post Office Box 322
3300 AH Dordrecht, THE NETHERLANDS

Library of Congress Cataloging-in-Publication Data
Pejovich, Svetozar.
  Economic analysis of institutions and systems / Svetozar Pejovich.
  -- Rev. 2nd ed.
      p. cm. -- (International studies in economics and
  econometrics ; v.3)
  Includes bibliographical references and index.
  ISBN 0-7923-8031-2
  1. Institutional economics. 2. Right of property. 3. Capitalism.
  4. Socialism. I. Title. II. Series.
  HB99.5.P45 1997
  330--dc21   97-34978
                                                                  CIP

Copyright © 1998 by Kluwer Academic Publishers

All rights reserved. No part of this publication may be reproduced, stored in a retrieval system or transmitted in any form or by any means, mechanical, photo-copying, recording, or otherwise, without the prior written permission of the publisher, Kluwer Academic Publishers, 101 Philip Drive, Assinippi Park, Norwell, Massachusetts 02061.

Printed on acid-free paper.

Printed in the United States of America

TO MY MOTHER

TABLE OF CONTENTS

Foreword		ix
Preface		xi

PART ONE:	THE FRAMEWORK FOR ECONOMIC ANALYSIS	1
Chapter 1	Important Concepts in Economics	3
Chapter 2	The Coase Theorem and Transaction Costs	9
PART TWO:	INSTITUTIONS, PROPERTY RIGHTS, AND SYSTEMS	21
Chapter 3	Institutions	23
Chapter 4	Law and Institutions	39
Chapter 5	Property Rights	57
Chapter 6	Capitalism and Socialism	71
PART THREE:	PROPERTY RIGHTS, EXCHANGE, AND PRODUCTION	95
Chapter 7	Private Property Rights, Exchange and Production	97
Chapter 8	Restrictions on Ownership, Exchange, and Production	111

Chapter 9	Free-Market Economies, the State, and Policy-Making	123
Chapter 10	Property Rights in Socialism, Exchange and Production	139
Chapter 11	Trade (Exchange), and Growth Under Different Institutional Arrangements	151

PART FOUR: PROPERTY RIGHTS AND BUSINESS FIRMS		165
Chapter 12	The Firm and Contracts	167
Chapter 13	Capitalist Firms	181
Chapter 14	Socialism: The Labor-Managed Firm	195
Chapter 15	Property Rights, Business Firms and Innovation	207
Index		215

FOREWORD

In the late 1980s, the field of comparative economics and NATO faced a similar problem: the threat of obsolescence. A predictable reaction of those who had made major investments in both comparative economics and NATO was to look for a new job. It was time to say: comparative economic systems are dead, long live comparative economic systems.

The purpose of this book is to redirect study of what we called comparative economic systems toward analysis of the development of institutions and the effects of alternative institutional arrangements on economic performance. To that end, the book internalizes into a theoretical framework (1) the effects of alternative property rights on the costs of transactions and incentives structures, (2) the effects of the costs of transactions and incentives on economic behavior, and (3) the evidence for refutable implications of those effects.

Analysis here focuses on the issues, propositions and conclusions that lend themselves to the only known scientific test: empirical verification. Thus, this book is not about what socialism or capitalism could have been, should have been, or should be. Nor is it an ode to capitalism. Its purpose is not to assert that capitalism is a better economic system than socialism. The history of this century and the market for institutions have done that. My purpose is to explain what is it that makes the institutions of capitalism better in terms of economic outcome than all other alternatives that have been tried since the beginning of recorded history.

The work continues to reveal my academic debt to Armen Alchian, James Buchanan, Douglass North, G. Warren Nutter, and Richard Posner. However, thanks to help, advice and criticism I have received from a number of scholars, this is much more than merely the second edition of the book I published in 1995.

I am truly grateful to Enrico Colombatto, Director of the International Centre for Economic Research in Turin, Italy, and to Jonathan Macey, J. Dupratt White Professor of Law and Director of the J. Olin Program in Law and Economics at Cornell Law School, for contributing chapters. Their contributions are significant additions. I am also grateful to John Moore, a life-long friend, for the preface, which sets the stage for analysis.

My colleague and friend Robert Ekelund, professor of economics at Auburn University has made two major contributions to this book. First, he helped me identify numerous inconsistencies and problem areas in the first edition. Second, the book Ekelund wrote with Robert Hebert, Robert Tollison, Gary Anderson and Audrey Davidson changed my views on and analysis of the rise of capitalism. Erick Weede from the University of Colon convinced me that my views on Max Weber's analysis of the importance of the Reformation on medieval spiritual and material life were certainly incomplete and likely wrong. Thrainn Eggertsson helped me understand better the importance of new institutional economics for the transition process in Eastern Europe. Robert Higgs' work on why the Great Depression lasted until well after the World War II ended changed a number of my perceptions. Doug Wills, a former student, suggested that the discussion of transaction costs should come early in the book. My students at Academia Istropolitana in Bratislava and at Texas A&M in College Station gave me much useful feedbacks on shortcomings of the first edition.

An opportunity to spend several months at the International Centre for Economic Research in Turin gave me a much needed opportunity to discuss my ideas with Angelo Petroni, a learned and perceptive philosopher of science from the University of Bologna. Once again, a grant from the Earhart Foundation gave me time to work on this book.

Sally Antrobus provided valuable editorial assistance. This time, I needed much less on-site technical support, giving my wife Susan a chance to pursue other activities.

Svetozar Pejovich
College Station

PREFACE

When I first began to teach in the field of comparative economic systems some thirty years ago, the textbooks and the methodology were mainly descriptive. We spent a great deal of time studying the institutional arrangements of the Soviet system of central planning (or central administration, as Eugene Zaleski insisted). We learned about the planning organs of French indicative planning, and we studied the selection and composition of the worker's councils in the Yugoslav self-management system. Most of efforts were devoted to these aspects; relatively little was spent analyzing the behavior of the individuals who inhabited these institutions.

In fact, there was a gulf between this field and the mainstream of economic analysis – in particular, the theories of price and markets. When the attention of most economists turned from market to non-market systems, the apparatus of neoclassical economics seemed powerless: no supply curves and no demand curves, at least not in the usual sense, and so applications of the standard methods simply could not be made. A few scholars ventured to apply utility-maximizing models in these circumstances,[1] but they represented a small minority. Much attention was paid to the *isms*; little to analysis.

Independent from the field of comparative economics but contemporaneously, new developments in economic theory were being made in the analysis of property rights. With the work of Coase, Alchian, Demsetz, and Manne, leading the way, breakthroughs in understanding how differing assignments of property rights, the costs of making transactions, the implications of alternative institutional arrangements, and so forth were made. The author of this volume, together with his colleague Eirik Furubotn, provided an invaluable survey and interpretation of this early work in a classic 1972 article.[2]

Property rights theory has had an enormous impact on economic analysis. It has greatly enriched the understanding of how ordinary

---

[1] Ward was one. See B. Ward, "Workers' Management in Yugoslavia," *Journal of Political Economy,* 65 (October,1957), pp. 373-85.
[2] E. Furubotn and S. Pejovich, "Property Rights and Economic Theory: A Survey of the Recent Literature," *Journal of Economic Literature* 10 (December, 1972), pp. 1137-62.

markets work and provided crucial insights into the characteristics of not-for-profit entities. It laid the basis for the new institutional economics. And it filled the gulf between standard, neoclassical economics and the study of non-capitalist forms of economic organization.

Steve Pejovich has been one of the leaders in applying the insights of property rights analysis and the new institutional economics to non-capitalist economic systems. His work on the self-managed firm as well as contributions regarding the Soviet economy have been highly significant in the shift away from the descriptive methods that characterized the field of comparative economic systems previously to the generalized analytical approach of today.

It is a regrettable fact of scientific research that the methods available at a time of great interest and gravity are not always the ones that are needed. This was surely true in the days of the old Soviet Union, when the insights of property rights analysis could well have led to more accurate prognoses. Those who believed in the heyday of the Soviet economy that its performance was both over-rated and certain to deteriorate were lonely voices indeed.[3] That new, general methods are available is perhaps even more important today, when the old "isms" have mostly disappeared, the remaining ones (such as China) are a complex blend of institutional forms, and when economic reforms and restructuring throughout the world are creating institutional singularities everywhere. It would be simply impossible, and surely foolish, to attempt to understand what is happening now in terms of any taxonomy. The new institutional economics, with its basis in property rights analysis, offers a powerful means of analyzing these new arrangements and making predictions about performance.

Thus the field of comparative economic systems has been revolutionized. This volume, the second edition of Pejovich's well-received book, can serve as a solid introduction to students interested in applying the new methods. More than that, it is an excellent guide to the economics of property rights and the application of the theory to market economic systems and the variety of institutional forms that exist in those systems. Its historical section serves to remind us that history does matter, that what has gone before conditions and helps to determine what is possible in the future, as the war in former Yugoslavia underscores so

---

[3] G. Warren Nutter was the most prominent lonely voice. See G. W. Nutter, *The Growth of Industrial Production in the Soviet Union, 1917-1959* (New York: National Bureau for Economic Research, 1962).

tragically. And it reminds us that economics, if it is not reduced to mere tautology, still does not explain everything.

John H. Moore
President, Grove City College.

PART ONE

THE FRAMEWORK FOR ECONOMIC ANALYSIS

Chapter 1

IMPORTANT CONCEPTS IN ECONOMICS

Ask yourself if there is something that you would like to have but have not been able to afford? Try asking your parents, friends, and even strangers. They will all agree that they have unsatisfied wants. Some of us may think that the very rich have everything. But we cannot be sure they have everything they want. They would probably say there are many things they want but have to do without. The message is simple. On the issues of aspirations, tastes, preferences, desires and feelings, we can only speak for ourselves. And speaking for ourselves, we all have unsatisfied wants.

The fact that we all have unsatisfied wants means that we live in a world of *scarcity*. Scarcity means that in order to get a little bit more of any good, a little bit of some of other good has to be given up. Every time I spend five dollars on a pastrami sandwich, I give up the satisfaction from another bundle of goods that five dollars could buy. A student deciding to study on a Saturday night gives up the satisfaction of going out on a date. No matter how affluent or poor we are as individuals, scarcity is always present; that is, what we want exceeds what is available.

The desire for more *utility* (satisfaction) is a behavioral consequence of the fact of scarcity. It predicts our behavior in a world in which what people want exceeds what they have. Economic analysis generalizes this behavior as demand for more utility.

All of human history is about our search for more utility. Individuals demand only those goods that give them utility or satisfaction. Anything that yields satisfaction to someone is then a good. It could be a physical object (a crystal vase), something to eat (ice cream), an activity (dating), or doing things for others (contributing to boy scouts). In the real world, individuals have diverse preferences, aspirations and values. They go on, day in and day out, learning about alternatives, interpreting them, and choosing those which they expect to make them better off. A greedy, rational, calculating "economic person" exists only in some obsolete books. Economics is about much more than just material things.

We satisfy wants by acquiring goods. But goods have to be produced. To produce goods we need to use a multitude of things including land, machines, people, raw materials, "gifts" of nature, and time (e.g., to develop a friendship). All those things become resources when we develop a desire for the goods they help to produce (e.g., oil had been known to American Indians for a long time before it became a resource). That is, resources are created. Once they are created, we search for more of them.

In addition to being scarce, resources have alternative uses. I can either work for the government or teach, but I cannot do both at the same time. You can always grow a little bit more food in your yard at the cost of having less lawn. A student could choose to study longer for a test in economics at the cost of giving up a bit of other activities that are also satisfying; a building could be used as a factory or residence; and so on. The point is that whenever we use resources to produce a little more of something, we are, in effect, choosing to produce less of something else. Next time your senator tells you that the state needs another highway, ask what it is that the taxpayers can do without.

Every time people decide to buy something, they have less income left for other things; and each time they choose to engage in an activity, they have less time for other activities. When a community decides to produce a few more cigars, it must give up something else that the same bundle of resources (land, machines, people, etc.) could have produced. We could get slightly cleaner air at a cost of reducing the supply of other goods (e.g., cars).

We can now define the concept of cost in economics. In a world of scarcity an increment in satisfaction from any good has its cost: *the value of that which is being given up, or the opportunity costs.*

The concept of opportunity costs explains the nature of human choices. Most human decisions are in terms of the marginal or incremental (more or less of A in exchange for less or more of other things), rather than the total (all or nothing of A). For example, from the standpoint of individual members of a community, the relevant criterion in making a choice on protection from crime, certainly a useful good, is the relationship between the incremental benefits from a little less crime and the incremental costs in terms of other things that have to be sacrificed. The issue is not one of crime or no crime.

THE NATURE OF ECONOMICS

Given that resources are scarce relative to human wants and are capable of alternative uses, all human societies--yesterday, today and tomorrow--have to resolve two fundamental survival issues: *who gets what* and *who does what.* The former is about the distribution of goods; each time an individual gets a bit of something, that much less is left for others. The latter is about production and innovation; every time we assign a resource to produce something, we are giving up a bundle of other things the same resource could have produced.

Economics seeks to identify circumstances that affect the costs of alternative choices, to analyze their implications for human decisions, and to make verifiable predictions about economic outcome. Economics, then, is the science of choice. It is a positive science; that is, economics does not judge human actions as good or bad, rational or irrational, desirable or undesirable.

To say that economics is a positive science means that it is about cognition rather than abstract valuations. Facts and observations have meaning only in the context of a theory, and the theory must be refutable. Economic theories are then generalized propositions of cause and effect. They must explain a wide class of real world events and yield observable propositions. *Ad hoc* theorizing has no scientific content.

INSTITUTIONS AND ECONOMIC PERFORMANCE

Recent years have seen a substantial increase in research on the relationship between institutions and economic performance. To incorporate the relationship between institutions and economic performance into a coherent and testable theory, it is necessary to show that (1) institutions have predictable effects on economic performance, and (2) changes in the social and economic conditions of life modify institutional arrangements.

The organization of this book reflects those two requirements for the development of a theory. Part two of the book analyzes institutions, property rights, and systems. Part three discusses the effects of alternative institutions on economic behavior. The final section explores the effects of alternative property rights on the choice of business firms, their performance, and incentives to innovate.

The book is about the theory of property rights, or--the same thing-- new institutional theory. Like all research efforts, this book reflects its author's understanding of the subject at hand. It is therefore helpful to begin with a few simple propositions in the economics of property rights.

1. The theory of property rights is a positive theory. It separates valuation from cognition. The late professor Karl Brunner focused on this

point in a number of his papers. He criticized scholars for marketing their own "values" to the public as if those values were cognitive statements about our world. The moral disaffection that some such scholars have for the prevailing social arrangements means only that they prefer another state of affairs to the one actually observed. Brunner wrote:

> The sacrifice of cognition is particularly easy to detect in objections to the market system introduced by discrepancies between one's desires, glorified as social values, and the results of market processes. However, our ability to visualize "better" states more closely reflecting our preferences yields no evidence that this state can be realized.[1]

The problem with abstract values is that they occur in a cognitive limbo. Thus, they provide no useful evidence for analysis. The relevant choice for a community is not between frictionless blackboard models of a "moral" society and the prevailing imperfect system. In a world of uncertainty and incomplete information, the only relevant choice is between imperfect systems.

2. The theory of property rights is a major departure from neoclassical economics. It is not the purpose of the book to denigrate a theory that has made numerous contributions to our understanding of social and economic issues. It is, however, important to understand how and why the theory of property rights differs from neoclassical economics. In the theory of property rights, the incentives effects of the rules of the game replace the maximization paradigm, and the feedback of their consequences on selection processes replaces the assumption of a rational agent who is able to identify the optimal strategy in each situation without any learning process. In fact, neoclassical economics is silent about both the effects of alternative rules on the agents' costs of acquiring the knowledge required to make optimal choices and the effects of new knowledge on prevailing rules. Schotter wrote:

> ...the only institutions existing in [the neoclassical model] are markets of the competitive type in which all information on the economy must be transmitted through the prices formed in these markets. The economy is therefore assumed to have ...none of the

---

[1] K. Brunner, "Knowledge, Values, and the Choice of Economic Organization," *Kyklos* 23 (1970), p. 563.

many social institutions that are created by societies to help coordinate their economic and social activities by offering information not available in competitive prices.[1]

3. The rational expectation theory and the principal-agent model bring the theory of property rights and neoclassical economics close to each other but not together. The rational expectation theory considers the process of adaptation to an optimal solution as a steady trial-and-error process in which the participants are not acquiring new knowledge. The principal-agent model defines a contractual relationship between a principal and an agent. The former employs the latter to perform a range of activities on his or her behalf. The costs of monitoring the agent being positive, the model seeks to reinstate an optimal solution through a contract that creates incentives for the agent to act in the principal's interest. The problem is that in a world of uncertainty and incomplete knowledge, not all future problems arising between the principal and the agent are pure risk decisions. Thus, the resolution of contingencies arising later between the two cannot depend on a contract but hinges upon the incentive effects of the prevailing rules. Herbert Simon wrote:

> [New economic theories] are not focused upon, or even much concerned with, how variables are equated at the margin, or how equilibrium is altered by marginal shifts in conditions. Rather they are focused on qualitative and structural questions, typically, on the choice among a small number of discrete institutional alternatives.[2]

4. The most critical concept upon which the theory of property rights rests is transaction costs. Given its relative newness, the concept of transaction costs is discussed in some detail in the next chapter.

---

[1] A. Schotter, "Why Take a Game Theoretical Approach to Economics," *Economie Applique* 36 (1983), p. 675.
[2] H. Simon, "Rationality as a Process and as a Product of Thought," *American Economic Review* 68 (1978), p. 6.

Chapter 2

THE COASE THEOREM AND TRANSACTION COSTS

Exchange and production (hereafter exchange) are the major methods by which people seek to resolve problems that have their source in scarcity.[1] The pursuit of exchange involves two levels of social activity. The first is the development, modification, and specification of institutions. The second level of social activity is exchange within the prevailing institutional arrangements. The former is about the rules of the game, while the latter is about the game itself.

The rules of the game are costly to produce. They are also costly to practice. Those costs are transaction costs. Transaction costs are the costs of all resources required for making an exchange (e.g., discovering exchange opportunities, negotiating exchange, monitoring, and enforcement), and for developing, maintaining, and protecting the institutional structure (e.g., judiciary, police, armed forces).

In the 1930s, Ronald Coase raised the issue of the importance of transaction costs for better understanding of social and economic processes. Slowly, academic research and empirical evidence confirmed Coase's contention that the total costs of an activity include both production *and* transaction costs. The post-1989 developments in Eastern Europe have made the importance of transaction costs in a world of uncertainty and different institutional arrangements quite obvious.

THE COASE THEOREM

Coase made two points: (1) clearly defined private property rights are an essential requirement for resolving the conflict of interests among individuals via market exchange, and (2) an efficient allocation of resources is independent of the initial assignment of property rights as long as transaction costs are insignificant. He wrote:

> [Individuals,] who are normally only interested in maximizing their own incomes, are not concerned with social cost and will only

---

[1] Strictly speaking production is also exchange.

10

undertake an activity if the value of the product of the factors employed is greater than their private cost....But if private cost is equal to social cost, it follows that [individuals] will only engage in an activity if the value of the product of the factors employed is greater than the value which they would yield in their best alternative use. That is to say, with zero transaction costs, the value of production would be maximized.[1]

Suppose that Hamilton and Jefferson are neighbors.[2] Their homes are next to each other and they have been getting along quite well. Hamilton and Jefferson value their homes at $1,200 and $1,000 respectively. These are subjective values that may but may not equal the market prices of the two homes.

One day, Jefferson gets an offer from Scream & Scare, Inc. to test sirens in his kitchen in exchange for $500. Being indifferent to noise, Jefferson gladly accepts the offer.[3] Testing sirens imposes a subjective cost on Hamilton, say $200. Thus, the values Jefferson and Hamilton place on their homes in the two situations are:

Table 2-1. The Coase Theorem

	Hamilton	Jefferson	Total Value
No sirens	$1,200	$1,000	$2,200
Sirens	$1,000	$1,500	$2,500

Testing sirens in Jefferson's home creates a new issue that did not exist before. Externality clearly exists because the cost borne by Hamilton does not enter into Jefferson's cost-benefit calculations.[4] Hamilton believes that he has the right not to suffer damages and wants Jefferson to stop testing sirens. Jefferson believes that testing sirens is a lawful activity and refuses to stop. Hamilton then takes Jefferson to court.

---

[1] R. Coase, "Notes on the Problem of Social Cost," in *The Firm, the Market, and the Law*, R. Coase, ed., (Chicago: University of Chicago Press, 1988), p. 158.
[2] I owe this method of explanation of the Coase Theorem to Professor Richard Adelstein.
[3] Assuming that Jefferson is indifferent to noise (for whatever reasons) does not change the results of our analysis, but eliminates the necessity of making an adjustment in his net gains from accepting the offer.
[4] It could if and when Jefferson considered the well-being of Hamilton as a good. Assuming that not to be the case simplifies our exposition of the Coase Theorem without changing its conclusions.

In order to internalize the costs and benefits from this new interdependence, the relevant property right must be defined. Before that is done, there is no way for Jefferson and Hamilton to negotiate a solution to their dispute. The relevant property right the court must determine is whether Hamilton has the right to impose additional costs on Jefferson by compelling him to stop testing sirens in his kitchen, or whether Jefferson has the right to impose additional costs on Hamilton by testing sirens in his kitchen. In short, the issue is who has the right of ownership in the noise from testing sirens in Jefferson's home.

Suppose Hamilton wins. Initially there will be no sirens. But the relevant property right is now defined. Jefferson knows that he is willing to offer up to $500 to purchase from Hamilton the right to continue testing sirens. While he might not know the value Hamilton places on that right, Jefferson has incentives to keep raising his offer until a deal is made. At some price between $200 and $500, exchange will happen. Suppose Jefferson buys the right for $300. Then, exchange between Hamilton and Jefferson has the following outcome:

> Sirens are going to be tested.
> Hamilton is worth $1,000 + 300 = $1,300; Jefferson is worth $1,500 - 300 = $1,200.
> The value of production is maximized at $2,500.
> The increment in total value of $300 ($2,500 - $2,200) is shared by Jefferson, who gets $200, and Hamilton, who gets $100.

Suppose Jefferson wins. Initially there are sirens. Driven by his self-interest, Hamilton has incentives to offer up to $200 to buy the right from Jefferson. However, Jefferson will accept no less than $500. With no opportunity for exchange between Hamilton and Jefferson, we have the following outcome:

> Sirens are tested.
> Hamilton is worth $1,000; Jefferson is worth $1,500.
> The value of production is maximized at $2,500.
> Jefferson gets $500 and Hamilton ($200) from the increment in total value of $300.

The sirens are tested regardless of the initial allocation of the relevant property right, and the total value is maximized ($2,500 vs. $2,200) either way. Hence, the Coase Theorem:

> Where bargaining is relatively costless, an efficient allocation of the relevant property right (i.e., the one that maximizes the value of production) will be achieved regardless of the initial allocation of that right. But the distribution of this maximized value will differ from one initial allocation to another.

What if transaction costs were positive? Assume that the state charges a sales tax of $700 for an exchange of the right to test sirens. If Hamilton wins, Hamilton is worth $1,200, Jefferson is worth $1,000, the value of production is *not* maximized at $2,200, and sirens are not tested because Jefferson cannot pay the minimum price of $200 plus the $700 tax.

However, if Jefferson wins, Hamilton is worth $1,000, Jefferson is worth $1,500, and the total value of production is maximized.

Hence, when transaction costs are positive and significant, the initial assignment of property rights matters. In general, with transaction costs being positive, efficiency will result only if the court grants the right to the highest-valued owner. In our example, the highest-valued owner is Jefferson.

TRANSACTION COSTS

The Coase Theorem says that the allocation of resources is independent of the legal assignment of property rights as long as transaction costs are insignificant. That is the world in which the costs of identifying, negotiating, and monitoring exchanges are negligible; the costs of protecting and maintaining the environment are ignored, and the maximum output is taken to be merely a function of the supply of inputs, their substitutability, and technology. However, the world of zero transaction costs is not the one we live in. It surely *is not* a Coasian world. Coase's purpose has been to persuade his colleagues to devote their energies to better understanding of the real world of uncertainty and incomplete knowledge. The relevant choice for policy is not between two or more frictionless models. The relevant choice is between two or more discrete institutional arrangements with positive transaction costs. Coase wrote:

> The reason why economists went wrong was that their theoretical system did not take into account a factor which is essential if one wishes to analyze the effect of a change in the law on the allocation of resources. This missing factor is the existence of transaction costs.[1]

Neoclassical economics is a product of the age of rationalism, with its conventional wisdom that *nature* had endowed individuals with reason capable of discovering and implementing efficient solutions to their existential problems. It summarizes the desire for more utility, a basic trait of observed human behavior, into the maximization paradigm, and analyzes economic outcomes of that behavior in a world of non-attenuated private ownership and insignificant transaction costs. Given the assumptions of non-attenuated private property rights and insignificant transaction costs, the maximization paradigm at the individual level assures an efficient outcome or equilibrium at the system level. By adjusting assumptions and constraints facing the individual decision maker, neoclassical economics has been able to identify a series of equilibria. All those equilibria are idealized statements about what the world would have been if uncertainty and incomplete knowledge were to go away.

Since its focus is on the end result of economic processes rather than the method of adaptation (why and how the observed patterns of behavior have emerged), neoclassical analysis is certainly not hostile to social engineering. Indeed, neoclassical economics has frequently been used to justify various public policies in a world of different institutional arrangements and varying transaction costs.

For example, studies in public finance often show the effects of various tax and public expenditure policies by moving the equilibrium solution for the economy (or a sector of the economy) along a given curve or by shifting that curve. The assumption behind this type of analysis is that the government is a cooperating agent in the model. Thus, changes in fiscal rules have no effect on incentives affecting transaction costs.

Studies in economic systems routinely compare equilibrium solutions based on neoclassical tools such as upward-sloping supply and downward-sloping investment schedules. The problem is that the slopes of those functions reflect the incentive effects of private property rights. That is, the supply schedule cannot be assumed to be upward sloping nor the

---

[1] R. Coase, *The Firm, the Market, and the Law*, p. 175.

investment schedule to be downward sloping in a non-private property economy. As we shall see later in this book, a state-owned firm induces different behavior than a privately owned firm. And even a privately owned firm in socialism induces behavior that is different than in capitalism.

A mechanical extension of neoclassical analytical concepts and tools to non-private property and/or positive transaction costs environments have produced misleading conclusions as well as policy prescriptions. Here are a few examples of pronouncements about the state of the Soviet economy as late as the 1980s.

Robert Heilbroner and Lester Thurow wrote: "Can economic command significantly compress and accelerate the growth process? The remarkable performance of the Soviet Union suggests that it can. In 1920 Russia was but a minor figure in the economic councils of the world. Today it is a country whose economic achievements bear comparison with those of the United States."[1] Paul Samuelson said: "It is a vulgar mistake to think that most people in Eastern Europe are miserable... The gap between Western and Eastern living standard may narrow in the future."[2] Seweryn Bialer and Joan Afferica wrote: "The Soviet Union is not now nor will it be during the next decade in the throes of a true systemic crisis, for it boasts enormous unused reserves of political and social stability that suffice to endure the deepest difficulties."[3] And John Kenneth Galbraith on his return from Russia in 1984 claimed that the Soviet economy had made great national progress in recent years.[4]

In the United States, the Securities and Exchange Commission, Federal Trade Commission, and many other regulatory organizations are an unintended consequence of using neoclassical economics to assure the economy of competitive outcomes. Demsetz wrote:

> The special notion of competition relied upon by the model [of perfect competition] makes that model a poor vehicle for understanding a wide variety of competitive tactics and institutions that are adopted precisely to accommodate ... uncertainty, and the

---

[1] R. Heilbroner, and L. Thurow, *The Economic Problem*, 7th edition, (Englewood Cliffs, NJ.: Prentice Hall, 1984), p. 629.
[2] P. Samuelson, *Economics*, 11th edition, (New York: McGraw Hill, 1980), p.824.
[3] S. Bialer and J. Afferica, "Reagan and Russia," *Foreign Affairs* 61 (Winter 1982-83), p. 263.
[4] J.K. Galbraith, "A Visit to Russia," *New Yorker* 60 (September 3, 1984), pp. 54-63.

cost of transacting. Particular marketing practices such as tie-in sales, reciprocity, and manufacturer control of prices at which retailers resell their goods are difficult to explain with a model that assumes away their cause. Vertical integration and the very existence of firms find little rationale in the perfect decentralization model because their source lies in the uncertainties of real economic systems and in the cost of rising markets to accommodate to these uncertainties.[1]

Examples of Transaction Costs

Information is not a free good. In a world of uncertainty and incomplete knowledge, it takes real resources (including time) to produce information. College graduates know that it takes time and money to gather information about employment opportunities, but the search costs might prevent them from discovering the best alternative. Shoppers know that by driving around they can find the best bargains, but it might not be an efficient thing to do given the cost of gasoline and the alternative uses for their time. However, if the price at which a person could obtain additional information were reduced, additional exchange opportunities would be exploited and the extent of exchange increased.

An important issue that underlies the theory of property rights is: What set of institutional arrangements encourages activities that reduce transaction costs? Or, what are the effects of various rules of the game on transaction costs?

In a private-property, free-market economy, resources are devoted to producing and selling information. Real estate agents, employment agencies, advertising, marriage and dating bureaus, and scalpers are all engaged in the production of transaction services. Stores maintain inventories because it is a method for protecting themselves against fluctuations in the demand for their goods (i.e., for reducing the cost of information). Sticky prices are a strategy on the part of the seller to purchase goodwill from buyers by reducing their costs of information about the terms of exchange over a period of transitory changes in demand.

---

[1] H. Demsetz, *Economic, Legal and Political Dimensions of Capitalism*, (Amsterdam: North Holland, 1982), p. 11.

The costs of *negotiating* exchange can be substantial. The parties may not know each other. They may not have all relevant information about goods and services. Goods and services have multiple attributes that are costly to measure. A consequence of measuring all those attributes would be a reduction in the extent of exchange. The extent of exchange would also be reduced if the allocation of risk and other future consequences of each and every exchange had to be negotiated separately.

Exchange is costly to *enforce*. Exchange can be simultaneous (e.g., buying fresh produce in a farmers' market) or it may take a period of time (e.g., I pay for my plane ticket before the airline fulfills its side of the bargain). In either case, but more clearly in the latter, misunderstandings concerning the attributes of goods, the bundle of rights being transferred, and delivery dates are to be expected. An enforcement mechanism reduces the cost of exchange, eliminates the time horizon problem, increases the extent of trade, and provides incentives for resources to move to their highest-valued uses.

The market provides an enforcement mechanism. Those who repeatedly fail to perform their side of the bargain lose business to their competitors. A reputable dealer gets a higher price for the same good or service than a fly-by-night operator. Thus, a good reputation is an asset that has monetary value. A newcomer in town must be willing to trade at a lower price while investing in developing a reputation. However, this selection process, important as it is, takes time and is costly. It is costly to many who act in good faith, to those who misunderstand the terms of exchange, and to the community as a whole because additional real resources have to be used to run credit bureaus, security deposits, and other means of self-protection.

Due to their stability and credibility, contractual agreements in the rule-of-law states reduce transaction costs by enforcing damages from breaches of contract, by preventing opportunistic behavior, and by reducing wasteful use of resources.

In *Alaska Packers' Association vs. Domenico*, the defendant hired a group of seamen to fish salmon off the coast of Alaska. The wages to be paid to the seamen were agreed to before the voyage. However, when the ship arrived in Alaskan waters, the seamen refused to work unless they were paid higher wages. Having no access to the labor market, the defendant agreed. But, upon return to San Francisco, he refused to pay his workers higher wages. The seamen sued and lost. The court held that the defendant's promise to pay the wages over and above the original contract was not supported by fresh consideration (reciprocal promise). This decision was efficiency-enhancing because it reduced incentives for opportunistic behavior by contractual partners. Richard Posner's comment on the court's decision in *Alaska Packers' Association vs. Domenico* was that once it was "well known that such modifications [in the contract] are unenforceable workers in the position of the seamen in the Domenico case will know that it will do them no good to take advantage of their employers' vulnerability."[1]

With a few exceptions, the law of contract allows each party to choose between performing in accordance with the contract or compensating the other party for damages. For example, A agrees to produce for B a number of computers. Then a better line of computers (produced by C) becomes available and the market for computers declines. Depending on costs, B can choose to cancel the contract and compensate A only for computers already produced and for other sustained costs. This is an efficiency-enhancing provision in the law of contract. B has to pay A for resources actually committed to production under their contract. The completion of computers that have become outdated would have used additional resources, which would be a waste.

Empirical Estimates of Transaction Costs

Douglas North and John Wallis made the first comprehensive effort to measure transaction costs.[2] As in many innovative works, for every answer it provided, the study raised new questions. Yet, North and Wallis gave us a method for measuring transaction costs as well as supplying incentives for further research.

The study has three parts. The first section develops a theoretical definition of transaction costs and the transaction sector. The gains from trade are a consequence of specialization and the division of labor. They are realized through exchange, which is not costless. An important implication is that transaction costs are a limiting factor on economic growth. It follows that incentives for efficiency improvements in the transaction sector are as important as

---

[1] R. Posner, *Economic Analysis of Law*, (Boston: Little, Brown, and Co. 1992), p. 87.
[2] J. Wallis and D. North, "Measuring the Transaction Sector in the United States Economy, 1870-1970," in *Long-Term Factors in American Economic Growth*, S. Engerman and R. Gallman, eds., (Chicago: University of Chicago Press, 1986), pp. 95-161.

those in the production sector. The issue (addressed in chapter 15) is which set of institutions provides incentives for innovation in the transaction sector of the economy.

The second part of the study provides empirical estimates of transaction costs in the United States economy for the period from 1870 to 1970. According to North and Wallis, transaction costs rose substantially during that period. Table 2-2 summarizes their empirical findings.

In the last section of the study, North and Wallis discuss potential implications of their empirical estimates of transaction costs. They offer three major explanations for the expansion of resources used in the transaction sector of a growing economy. First, the expansion of markets and growing urbanization of the economy replaces repeated dealing with contractual partners we know with an ever-lengthening chain of exchanges carried out between individuals who have no knowledge of each other. Impersonal exchange requires more information-gathering activity as well as more elaborate enforcement mechanisms.

Table 2-2. The Transaction Sector as a Percentage of GNP in the USA

Year	Private Sector	Public Sector	Total
1870	22.49	3.60	26.09
1880	25.27	3.60	28.87
1890	29.12	3.60	32.72
1900	30.43	3.67	34.10
1910	31.51	3.66	35.17
1920	35.10	4.87	39.98
1930	38.19	8.17	46.35
1940	37.09	6.60	43.69
1950	40.30	10.95	51.25
1960	41.30	14.04	55.35
1970	40.80	13.90	54.71

Source: Wallis and North, "Measuring the Transaction Sector in the United States Economy, 1870-1970," p. 121.

Second, capital-intensive production techniques increase incentives for business enterprises to grow in size. An implication is that more resources have to be devoted to transaction services within the firm. Finally, the gains from trade tend to create conflicting interpretations about the prevailing institutional arrangements as well as about the justice and fairness of the distribution of income in general and the increments of income in particular. Whether those conflicts emerge from differences in customs, ethnicity, religion and race or from occupational specialization and loss of personalized relationships between individuals in the community, more resources have to be devoted to defining and enforcing the rules of the game.

SUGGESTED READING

A. Alchian, "Some Implications of Property Rights Transaction Costs," in *Economics and Social Institutions,* K. Brunner, ed. (Boston: M. Nijhoff, 1977).

R. Coase, "The Problem of Social Cost," *Journal of Law and Economics* 3 (1960).

PART TWO

INSTITUTIONS, PROPERTY RIGHTS, AND SYSTEMS

Chapter 3

INSTITUTIONS

The transaction costs of making contracts credible are positive. In order to control those costs, people develop rules. As we have observed earlier, social activity involves human interactions at two levels. The first is the development and maintenance of institutions, while the second is about human interactions within the prevailing institutions. The former is about the rules of the game, while the latter is about the game itself.

The rules are necessary in a world of uncertainty and incomplete knowledge. They arise from the complexity of the environment; the computational limitations of the individual to understand, process, and utilize information about that environment; and the importance of predicting the behavior of contractual partners. Individuals' perceptions of the real world, then, are colored by their values, experiences, traditions, observed successes and failures, and reason. Dedication to ideologies, sacrifice in defense of abstract causes, depth of religious beliefs, and many other observed behaviors of individuals and groups can be neither ignored nor dismissed as ad hoc events.

Given their subjective perceptions of reality, individuals develop institutions or rules of the game. *We define institutions as the legal, administrative and customary arrangements for repeated human interactions.* Their major function is to enhance the predictability of human behavior.

The prevailing institutional framework in a society consists of formal and informal rules. Formal rules are constitutions, statutes, common laws, and other governmental regulations which are externally enforced. They define the political system (the hierarchical structure, decision-making powers, the individual's rights); the economic system (property rights in scarce resources, contracts); and the protection system (judiciary, police, military). Informal rules have their origins in the experiences, traditional values, customs, religious beliefs, ethnicity and other factors that influence the subjective perceptions individuals form to interpret reality.[1] They are part of the heritage or culture, transmitted from one generation to another via teaching and imitation. That is why informal rules are called the ethos. We define *ethos* as the observed pattern of behavior that emerges from the interaction between the prevailing ethics and the conditions for survival as those are perceived by the community.

STABLE AND CREDIBLE INSTITUTIONS

A major function of the rules of the game is to reduce the transaction cost of human interactions through making human behavior predictable. To accomplish this objective, institutions must be credible (i.e., enforced) and stable.

Credibility (Enforcement) of Institutions

Rules that are loosely enforced do not encourage human interactions and cease to be a predictor of human behavior. The result is higher transaction costs of exchange and fewer exchanges. From an individual standpoint, rules yield a flow of benefits. The source of those benefits is the predictability of other people's behavior. My knowledge that other drivers will stop at a red light is my benefit from the rule. Rules are also costly. The cost of a rule (formal or informal) is the satisfaction a person has to give up by not being able to engage in the activity which the rule constrains. The fact that I must stop at a red light is the cost I bear.

It is essential for both economic growth and social stability of the community to develop and enforce institutional structures that provide incentives for individuals to seek contracts with other individuals far removed from their personal knowledge, or extending over long periods of time, or both.[2]

---

[1] R. Boyd and P.J. Richerson, *Culture and Evolutionary Process*, (Chicago: Chicago University Press, 1985), p. 2.
[2] D. North, "Institutions, Economic Growth, and Freedom," in *Freedom, Democracy, and Economic Welfare*, M. Walker, ed. (Vancouver: Fraser Institute, 1988), pp. 5-7.

Stability of Institutions

As time goes by, individuals become better acquainted with the rules. They learn how to adjust to the system, identify exchange opportunities, and exploit the most beneficial ones. Thus, the flow of benefits from institutions depends on their stability. For example, as long as university X has a well-defined set of rules, seniors are likely to capture more benefits from those rules than are sophomores. If the school changed its rules every year, the never-ending process of "learning" them would reduce their flow of benefits for all students.

The purchase of land, investments in various assets, and many other exchange opportunities have long-run consequences. Frequent changes in or expectations about changes in the rules of the game tend to increase the risk and uncertainty associated with those decisions, and such factors raise the costs of exchange relative to those in contractual agreements that have a shorter time horizon. Jews in medieval Europe favored investments in jewelry, gold coins, and other liquid assets. South Americans prefer lower rates of return from investments in the United States to the much higher rates of return that are often available in their homelands. An investor in post-communist Russia seeks a shorter payoff period than that available in Germany. A stable and credible set of rules provides incentives to create new knowledge about exchange opportunities, and to exploit the most beneficial ones regardless of their time horizons.

In a recent study, Robert Higgs presented convincing evidence that by denting investors' confidence in the stability of private property rights, the New Deal contributed significantly to prolonging the Great Depression until after World War II ended. He said:

> From 1935 through 1940, with Roosevelt and the ardent New Dealers who surrounded him in full cry, private investors dared not risk their funds in the amount typical of the late 1920s. In 1945 and 1946, with Roosevelt dead, the New Deal in retreat, and most of the wartime controls being removed, investors came out in force.[1]

---

[1] R. Higgs, "Regime Uncertainty: Why the Great Depression Lasted So Long and Why the Prosperity Resumed after the War," *The Independent Review* 1, 4 (1997), p. 587.

Comparison with a football game may illustrate the consequences of unstable institutions. In football, the rules of the game are set. Fans enjoy watching the game. Players know how to play it. And coaches know how to prepare their players. However, during an important game the blue team is on the one-yard line and fails to execute the fourth down. The coach goes to the referee and pleads: "My players worked so hard to get to the goal line, please give them another down?" Suppose the referee has power to choose to go along with the request, and the blue team scores. In the short run the blue team has won. But frequent changes in the rules would raise the costs of the game downstream. Football fans would not be able to enjoy the game, players would not know how to prepare for it, and football clubs would seek coaches who are better at getting rules changed than at coaching the players.

DEVELOPMENT OF INSTITUTIONS

Informal Institutions

Human life in primitive society was geared toward the search for subsistence in its natural state. In the pursuit of subsistence, small bands were formed. The survival of small bands depended on cooperation among members. Eventually, rules of behavior emerged within small groups.

Those rules were not simply a product of human reason--many social animals also evince rules affecting individuals' behavior, evolved as survival mechanisms within groups--although reason can explain their consequences. Human interactions that demonstrated survival traits were repeated, and the behaviors that passed the test of time were institutionalized into taboos, traditions, routines, beliefs, culture, and all other perceptions of the world. Those rules are called informal institutions. Predictably, different groups ended up with different informal institutions.

The informal institutions of a group are that group's repository of survival behaviors. The ethos is transmitted from one generation to another by imitation and in the context of stories about the life of the group. It is also modified in response to changes in the conditions of life. An interesting observation by Friedrich Engels, the closest collaborator of Karl Marx, speaks of one such change in informal rules.

> To the barbarian of the lower stage...human labor still does not produce any considerable surplus over its maintenance costs.... The [prisoners of war] were killed or adopted into the tribe.... After the introduction of cattle breeding, weaving, and agriculture...prisoners of war were turned into slaves.[1]

Members of small groups lived together and interacted with one another. Interactions with members of other groups were rare and might not have been very friendly, but within the group, the transaction costs of monitoring and enforcing informal rules were low. The costs an individual had to bear for violating informal rules (as is still so today) ranged from having to put up with unhappy neighbors to being expelled from the community.

In time, the development of new trade routes and general improvements in knowledge created opportunities for individuals in a given community to interact with members of other communities. To capture the potential gains from exchange, members of the group had to enter into contracts with individuals whom they did not know, who followed different customs, and whose behavior they could not observe at a low cost. That is, new opportunities did emerge, but the transaction costs of exploiting them were high and often prohibitive. To realize potential gains, the transaction costs of enforcing inter-community contracts had to be reduced.

Pursuing their self-interest, kings, feudal lords, and bishops in Europe rose to the challenge by (1) integrating local customs with the rules derived from Christian ethics, (2) providing protection for travelers, and (3) offering credible protection of property rights; that is, competition between semi-autonomous feuds gave incentives to feudal lords to provide credible guarantees of property rights.

As transaction costs of exploiting new opportunities fell, the extent of exchange increased. Kings, lords, and bishops claimed a share of the gains from the resulting economic growth. More exchanges, in turn, created new knowledge about economic opportunities and reinforced economic growth, leading eventually to a

---

[1] F. Engels, *The Origin of the Family, Private Property, and the State* (New York: International Publishers, 1942), pp. 58 and 65.

change in the balance of power between semi-autonomous city-states and the central power, in favor of the latter.

Nowadays, commercial laws provide the same service. By incurring the costs of enforcing contracts between total strangers (cotton produced in Australia might be used to make shirts in New York which are then sold to ranchers in Montana), governments create opportunities for the growth of wealth and appropriate a share of those gains through taxation.

In general, informal institutions emerge spontaneously. And they make a difference. Similar formal rules in the Untied States and many South American countries have produced different outcomes, because the informal rules differ. Privatization laws in post-1989 Eastern Europe are having different results from one country to another. Japanese culture has survived American commercial influence. Serbs preserved their customs through five centuries of Turkish formal rules. Many "boat people" in the United States have prospered under a set of formal rules they could not possibly have understood upon their arrival. And in Shasta County, California, the residents rely on a set of informal rules rather than on legal norms to resolve disputes arising from damages done by stray livestock[1]

Formal rules can suppress but they cannot chase out informal rules. Formal and informal rules coexist either in harmony (e.g., a rule protecting one's reputation) or in conflict (e.g., the prohibition laws of 1920s).

Many informal rules have evolved into their present form from serving a once important purpose. The convention of showing an open hand when greeting a stranger, at one time, served to show that one was not bearing a weapon. The caste system in India has survived its origin, which was to enhance the division of labor in labor-intensive agriculture. To paraphrase North, informal rules matter because the present and the future are connected to the past by the continuity of a society's institutions even after they outlive their usefulness.

---

[1] R. Ellickson, "Of Coase and Cattle: Dispute Resolution Among Neighbors in Shasta County," *Stanford Law Review*, 38 (1986), pp. 624-87.

Formal Institutions

Friedrich Hayek generalized the history and development of formal institutions into the continental or rationalistic tradition on the one hand, and the British or empirical tradition on the other. The former emphasized exogenous or outcome-oriented rules, which emerge mostly in the political domain, while the accent of the latter was on endogenous or incremental rules which, emerge spontaneously through repeated interactions.

Outcome-Oriented Changes

The continental tradition had two tenets: There exists a just society in which people can live in peace and harmony, and human reason is capable of discovering the institutions required to bring about such a society. The continental tradition provided the philosophical rationale and political justification for governments to develop and impose outcome-oriented (exogenous) rules of the game.

The continental tradition encouraged systematic investment in knowledge supportive of outcome-oriented rules. Antitrust laws, labor laws, and regulatory agencies such as the Federal Trade Commission are a few examples of such developments in the United States. In the 1990s research institutes and teaching centers, most of them financed by European taxpayers, have been set up all over Europe with the objective of creating knowledge supportive of the European Union.

Exogenous changes in the rules are usually conceptualized by scholars, advocated by various pressure groups, designed by lawyers, enacted by elected officials, and carried out by bureaucrats. It would not be fair to say that social engineers do not have good intentions. But the changes they advocate rely, for better or worse, on the strong hand of the state to force the game to adjust to new rules. And the changes are justified by reference to justice, fairness, morality, and/or the public interest. The problem with these terms is that none of them has a well-defined (agreed upon) empirical content. If we assume that presidents Clinton and Reagan both acted in good faith, the public interest is surely a very elusive concept. That is, the public interest is defined by individuals who, like all other individuals, have their own preferences, values, and private ends.

Using history as a guide, we can identify three general approaches to exogenous institutional changes: holistic, utopian, and incremental.

Holists tend to generalize historical events and personalities into prophesying the direction of social and economic development in society. Hence, why not give the community a push in the right direction? Examples of holists are Hegel, Marx, and the German Historical School. A holistic approach to social restructuring can easily be radicalized, as by Lenin, Stalin, Mao and Castro.

Utopians believe that we can use reason to discover the "just" society. Critical requirements that utopians have to deal with are: (1) Who is to identify the just outcome? (2) What kinds of institutions would channel human behavior in the direction of that outcome? (3) How are competing institutions to be suppressed without eliminating democracy? Examples of utopians are pre-Marx socialists, the political elite in most Third World countries, and supporters of the so-called industrial democracy in the West.

Incrementalists seek to restructure society by way of marginal changes in the rules of the game. Examples include hiring quotas, minimum wage laws, etc.

The common belief of all advocates of exogenous institutional changes is that the price of social restructuring is worth paying. It is important to understand that the issue is not whether exogenous changes can do good. They can and have at times produced good outcomes. The issue is that they create a window of opportunity for public decision makers to satisfy their vision of a *good* community at the expense of its members. The late professor Warren Nutter used to define the objectives of social and economic engineering as a hazy vision of things that would be nice to have.

Spontaneous Changes

The British tradition grew out of a strong dose of skepticism toward either the rulers' foresight or their goodwill or both. It questioned the conventional prescription of good government, which is to seek and elect good leaders and give them the power to do what is right. To paraphrase William Niskanen, the British tradition held that in a world of uncertainty and incomplete knowledge, good leaders do not assure good government, high purpose does not assure good law, and good analysis does not assure good policy.[1] The rules do.

Instead of searching for institutions that are outcome-oriented, the British tradition emphasized the right of individuals to pursue their private ends. The rules of the game then emerge spontaneously via repeated voluntary interactions. Because of their voluntary acceptance, endogenous rules are self-sustaining. The role of the state is (1) to monitor and enforce those rules--a role not too different from that of the referee in a football game, and (2) to institutionalize repeated interactions into the law.

The British tradition, then, advocates rules of the game that are the result of a process of selective evolution, and which maintain themselves by incremental adaptation to changes in the social and economic conditions of life. Individuals accept those rules not because they understand them but because the rules work. Professor Angelo Petroni from the University of Bologna wrote:

> The fact that the mechanism of evolution, when large numbers and long periods of time are involved, may be treated by the economist as if it were a Darwinian one, does not imply that individuals do not have a purposive objective-seeking behavior including imitation of others' successful behavior.[2]

The prevailing set of institutions in any society is a mix of spontaneous and exogenous rules. The preponderance of one or another type of formal institutions determines the opportunity set of the ruling elite. Spontaneous institutions raise the costs to the members of the ruling elite of pursuing their private ends. Outcome-oriented rules create opportunities for rent-seeking coalitions to be formed. While it is not always easy to determine whether an institution is endogenous or exogenous, a helpful hint is that institutions that emerge spontaneously tend to be noncompulsory (e.g., the rule of limited liability, stock exchanges). However, some endogenous rules are mandatory, like driving on the right-hand side of the road.

---

[1] W. Niskanen, "Public Policy and the Political Process," in *Governmental Controls and the Free Market*, S. Pejovich ed. (College Station: Texas A&M University Press), p. 76.

[2] A. Petroni, "What is Right with Hayek's Ethical Theory?" Paper presented at the Mont Pelerin Society meeting in Cannes, September 25-29, 1994, p. 26.

Both traditions confirm the old dictum that ideas have consequences. The continental tradition created the market for social engineering and contributed, perhaps unintentionally, to the rise of socialism. The British tradition made a major contribution to the rise of classical liberal philosophy and methodological individualism.

THE DIRECTION OF CHANGE

The agent of the process of change is the individual. In the pursuit of their private ends, individuals compete for scarce goods. The competition is carried out by means of institutions, the critical function of which is to reduce the costs of exchange and production.

The competitive process is a *knowledge-creating process*. It means that competition continuously develops new opportunities for exchange, creates new resources, discovers new sources of supplies, invents new technology, and brings about changes in individuals' subjective perceptions of reality. In order to capture the potential gains from this never-ending process of creating new knowledge, individuals and organizations have to seek and negotiate new types of contracts. If the prevailing rules were poorly attuned to such contracts, observed exchanges between interacting individuals would approach the margin of accepted behavior. That is, the demand for adjusting the rules to the requirements of the game would arise from within the system.

Given potential gains from exploiting new opportunities, individuals have incentives to negotiate contracts that are submarginal in terms of the prevailing ethos. If operating below the margin of accepted behavior provided a differential return, the success of those individuals--whether we call them innovators, speculators, sleazes or whatever term suits one's preferences--would attract competition from others. If the returns were substantial enough to generate and sustain a large number of repeated interactions, the prevailing institutions would slowly but surely adjust to the new requirements of the game.

The demand for institutional change has to be effective; that is, those who stand to gain from changes in the rules must be willing to bear the costs of restructuring. And the cost of institutional restructuring can be high. Changes in formal rules may require a costly effort in terms of time and resources (including overcoming of the free-rider problem). Changes in informal rules are costly because of their tenacity. It takes time for informal rules to change.

For example, changes in the opportunity costs (i.e., relative price) of being a homemaker in the United States led to a significant increase in women's participation in the labor force. A critical factor affecting the opportunity costs of staying at home was the growth of output coupled with an enormous increase in the range of durable consumer goods. In order to capture potential gains from joining the labor force, women had to press for changes in a number of the prevailing formal and informal rules supporting the traditional family. In the traditional family husbands specialized in earning incomes, while wives specialized in homemaking and raising children. Men bragged about their affairs while wives hid these even from their best friends. Single women were socially marginalized. Wives went to work in order to pay some specific bills, between pregnancies, and after kids went to college.

The response of the competitive market for labor was predictable. Given high information costs of identifying career-oriented women, the competitive labor market treated all women as a high-cost resource relative to men. Pressures on legislators from various feminists groups, which identified the resulting income differences with discrimination based on sex, to equalize money incomes of men and women could have only raised the transaction costs of monitoring and enforcing employment contracts without solving the real issue. The competitive market for labor was not discriminating; it was responding to the prevailing rules. The real issue was to remove the constraints of informal and formal rules, so that the competitive market for labor would have no reason to differentiate between men and women.

With some women earning differential returns at the cost of social ostracism, the pressure for changes in the rules came from within the system, and the rules eventually adjusted to the new requirements of the game. We observe changes in informal rules such as the social acceptance of the Pill, of single motherhood and of live-in arrangements. We also observe changes in formal rules, including abortion laws and simplified divorce proceedings. Those changes in the rules of the game slowly but surely have been providing women with opportunities to compete in the labor market as equal to men.

There are then basically three ways for the community to respond to a demand for a change in the rules of the game.

(1) Allocative efficiency method refers to adjustments within the prevailing institutional framework. We observe this method of responding to demand for changes in the rules whenever the prevailing

establishment has greater bargaining strength than those who expect to profit from institutional changes. A good example is Gorbachev's attempts to save the Soviet system. It is a good example because it also shows that even the top leader of the most tightly controlled society in the entire history of mankind had to make his decisions in a world of uncertainty and incomplete knowledge.

(2) Adaptive efficiency method is to allow individuals and organizations to seek and negotiate new kinds of contracts and then to institutionalize those that are repeatedly observed. Changes in the rules are both incremental and spontaneous, and they occur in response to changes in the requirements of the game. Lance Davis and Douglass North remarked: "It is the possibility of profits that cannot be captured within the existing arrangemental structure that leads to the formation of new (or the mutation of old) institutional arrangements."[1]

In a groundbreaking study, Gary Libecap analyzed the development of mineral laws in the western United States in the second half of the nineteenth century.[2] A major problem at that time was the inability of the then prevailing institutions to take advantage of the rising value of mineral resources. That is, the rules of the game were not attuned to new demands of the game. Libecap found that the development of mineral law in the American West responded to changes in the requirements of the game. The rising value of mineral deposits created potential benefits. The exploitation of those benefits required the development of a bundle of property rights that was better attuned to new requirements of the game. The fact that new property rights developed means that potential benefits from mining were judged to be in excess of the costs of defining and enforcing those rights. Libecap concluded the study saying:

> The last half of the nineteenth century in the American West was a time of intense economic and legal change, as the mining industry boomed, spurred by huge ore discoveries...pressure on existing legal institutions...forced new ownership structure to

---

[1] L. Davis, and D. North, *Institutional Change and American Economic Growth*, (Cambridge: Cambridge University Press, 1971), p. 59.
[2] G. Libecap, "Economic Variables and the Development of the Law: The Case of Western Mineral Rights," in *Empirical Studies in Institutional Change*, L. Alston, T. Eggertsson, and D. North eds. (Cambridge: Cambridge University Press, 1966), pp. 34-58.

emerge. This resulted in the observed progression in mineral rights law from general, unwritten rules in the 1850s to highly specified statutes and court verdicts by the end of the century....The historical record and the statistical tests suggest that the evolution of mineral rights law in Nevada can be understood as an adjustment process to reduce ownership uncertainty.... Since there was little existing mineral law to borrow from (either state or federal), most of the Nevada statutes and court verdicts were written in response to local conditions.[1]

(3) Piecemeal social engineering method of responding to demand for institutional restructuring requires the government purposefully to design and implement changes in the rules. The results of using piecemeal social engineering depend on the balance of bargaining power between the establishment on the one hand and individuals and organizations demanding a change in the rules on the other. Changes in the rules are incremental but not spontaneous. A good example is the development of telecommunications in the United States and Western Europe. US rules were plastic enough (e.g., as in the breakup of AT&T) to encourage individuals and groups to explore alternative ways of exploiting new technological opportunities. Consequently, the system moved in the direction of adaptive efficiency. In Europe, the establishment had much greater bargaining strength and the system moved in the direction of piecemeal social engineering. However, most recent developments in Europe suggest that the results of the competitive process in the United States have been noticed.

WHY DO INSTITUTIONS DIFFER?

Our discussion does not suggest the existence of a mechanism for replacing less efficient institutions with more efficient ones. And for a good reason. We do not observe such a tendency in the real world. We observe the growth of institutional arrangements that enhance the growth of wealth. We also observe the growth of rules that restrict exchange and production. How do we explain the fact that more

---

[1] G. Libecap, "Economic Variables," p. 57.

efficient institutions have failed to drive less efficient ones out of existence? Why do less efficient institutions manage to survive?

One reason is self-interest of the political elite. Members draw their power and rewards from the prevailing rules. To preserve their position and status, members of the political elite have incentives to create rent-seeking opportunities for a segment of the community that might, in turn, support the prevailing regime. The method of forming rent-seeking coalitions might take different forms in different communities depending on perceptions by the political elite of the prevailing balance of power. We observe research grants for educators, higher than necessary military budgets, business regulations favoring established firms, support for labor unions, and foreign trade restrictions, among many other forms. The objective of the political elite is always the same: to get a critical number of powerful groups to support the prevailing system. And as long as members of the community perceive the resulting inefficiencies of the system to be less than the costs of changing the system, the prevailing system will continue to exist with, at best, small marginal changes.

Second, in free societies, people respond to opportunities for exchange by trying different types of contracts. The collective set of actual choices then approximates a random selection of contractual arrangements, from which successes and failures are chosen. With uncertainty and incomplete information, individuals interpret the results of different types of contracts differently. This means that all arrangements producing positive gains--rather than the most efficient one--are eligible for imitation. The convergence to the most efficient institutional arrangement would require a process during which no new knowledge is created, and no new issues requiring changes to the prevailing rules emerged. Armen Alchian wrote:

> [I do] not regard uncertainty as an aberrational exogenous disturbance, as does the usual approach from the opposite extreme of accurate foresight. The existence of uncertainty and incomplete information is the foundation of...analysis; the importance of the concept of a class of "chance" decisions rests upon it; it permits of various conflicting objectives; it motivates and rationalizes a type of adaptive behavior; yet it does not destroy the basis of prediction, explanation, or diagnosis. It does not base its aggregate description on individual optimal

action; yet it is capable of incorporating such activity where justified.[1]

Transaction costs of institutional restructuring are another reason why less efficient institutions continue to survive. The sources of those transaction costs are both subjective and objective. The former include the individual's perception of reality, which is shaped by the prevailing institutional framework. The latter are sunk investments in the prevailing set of formal and informal rules, the bargaining strength of the establishment, and imperfect markets.[2] An implication is that people have incentives (except in the case of a major change in relative prices) to make marginal adjustments in the prevailing rules rather than to incur the costs of institutional restructuring. Indeed we observe communities all over the world moving along inefficient (dependency) paths even though aware of more efficient institutional structures elsewhere.

Finally, by linking their present functions with originating circumstances, institutions give the hand of the past continuing leverage on the present. They become the *carriers of history*. Paul David addressed the issue of the tenacity of institutions as follows:

> I perceive there to be three main analytical insights concerning the roots of path-dependence in economic phenomena which can take us a long way toward understanding why history matters so vitally where human organizations and institutions are concerned. The first has to do with the role of historical experience in the formation of structures of mutually consistent expectations that enable coordination to be achieved without centralized direction of the individual economic agents. The second is concerned with ...the resemblance between the information channels and codes that organizations require in order to function with even a minimum level of economic efficiency. The third involves ...the necessity of achieving consistency and compatibility among the constituent elements of human organizations.[3]

---

[1] A. Alchian, "Uncertainty, Evolution, and Economic Theory," *Journal of Political Economy* 58 (1950), p. 221.
[2] D. North, Institutions, Institutional Changes, chapter 11.
[3] P. David, "Why Are Institutions the 'Carriers of History'?" Paper presented at the Stanford Institute Symposium on "Irreversibilities," July 1992, p. 6.

Professor David's second point is especially interesting. It says that organizations develop their own "cultures," which have all the characteristics of capital assets specific to those organizations. For example, an engineer working for Texas Instruments has to master the firm's culture, which includes communication channels, information-processing procedures, and other internal codes. The employee's knowledge of the Texas Instruments culture, which is of little value elsewhere, becomes part of the firm's capital stock. Both the firm and the employee have incentives to maintain this culture into the future.

SUGGESTED READING

Alchian, A. "Uncertainty, Evolution and Economic Theory," *Journal of Political Economy* 58 (1950).

D North, *Institutions, Institutional Changes and Economic Performance,* (Cambridge: Cambridge University Press, 1990).

Chapter 4

LAW AND INSTITUTIONS

The rule of law means absence of arbitrary power on the part of the ruling group; subjection of all citizens to the same laws; stable and credible rules; and democratic elections. The absence of discretionary power means that no rule is to be enacted with the intent of helping or harming particular individuals. Equality before the law means that all citizens, including members of the ruling group, are subject to the same laws administered by independent courts. Stable and credible rules enhance social stability. Democratic elections mean that the ruling elite can be replaced by a simple majority at regularly scheduled elections. An implication is that the political elite has incentives to satisfy preferences of the median voter on key issues.

On the strict interpretation of the rule of law no country would qualify. However, the concept of the rule of law provides an ideal yardstick for comparison of alternative institutions and their economic, political and social consequences. The further a country travels away from the rule of law the greater the power of the ruling group to create institutions that strengthen and perpetuate its own powers. Walter Williams wrote:

> Fascism, communism and socialism are kindred forms of collectivism whose survival critically depends upon undermining of private property rights, rule of law, limited government and other institutions. Collectivists everywhere disdain the rule of law, traditions and the market place in favor of the direct pursuit of intended outcomes.[1]

The subjection of every individual to the ordinary law before courts, as in the British tradition (inherited by the United States), means that all citizens, including high level officers of the state are subject to the same laws as administered by ordinary and independent courts. The

---

[1] W. Williams, "Liberals Care Only About Results," Conservative Chronicle, February 9, 1994, p. 24.

continental tradition is somewhat different. Special administrative courts are often given the power of deciding the cases between private citizens and state officials when the latter are acting in their official capacity. A potential danger of this arrangement is that it might create an opportunity for officials to identify their side of the issue with the public interest.

The constitution is the highest law in a rule of law state. Its critical function is to protect individual rights from the majority rule. To paraphrase Buchanan, the rule of law means that the term constitution comes before the term democracy. He said:

> If individual liberty is to be protected, ...constitutional limits must be in place prior to and separately from any exercise of democratic governance.... An understanding of priorities in this respect should, of course, offer the basis for an extension of constitutional constraints on majoritarian legislative processes in modern polities and notably with reference to potential monetary and fiscal exploitation, quite apart from the more obvious "taking" activity that must everywhere be condemned.[1]

While constitutional principles are firmly embedded in the West, their legal origins differ in the British and continental systems. The British tradition generalizes the principles of the constitution from specific decisions (precedents) entered by common law courts. As old precedents are dropped and new ones are added to the legal system, judge-made rules change the constitution *incrementally*. Once the basic law of the land had been enacted in 1776, the United States accepted the British tradition for constitutional changes. Evidence is the importance of decisions (precedents) entered by common law courts, and the very costly method for changing the United States constitution. Judge Posner explained the production of precedents as follows:

> When a case is decided, the decision is thereafter a precedent, i.e. a reason for deciding a similar case the same way. While a single precedent is a fragile thing...an accumulation of

---

[1] J. Buchanan, *Property as a Guarantor of Liberty* (Aldershot, England: Edward Elgar Publishing, 1993), p. 59.

precedents dealing with the same question may create a rule of law having the same force as an explicit statutory rule....the body of precedents in an area of law is a stock of capital goods that yields services over many years to potential disputants in the form of information about legal obligations....The capital stock of precedents is the joint product of the lawyers and judges engaged in the argument and decision, respectively, of cases, mainly appellate cases....As old precedents reach obsolescence, eventually ceasing to be a part of the usable stock of precedents, new ones are added to the stock through litigation.[1]

In the continental tradition, precedents have only indirect bearing. The principles of the constitution are written by experts, debated by groups of citizens, and eventually adopted by constitutional assemblies or regular parliaments. The rights and liberty of individuals are then deduced from the general principles of the constitution. Parliaments have the power to modify the prevailing constitution and even replace it with another. The requirement that a change in the constitution must be supported by a constitutional majority protects individuals from simple majority rule. Yet, relative to the British tradition, where changes in the rules are incremental and tied to changes in the game, the continental tradition gives the political elite more room for discrete changes in the constitution. An implication is that the costs of long-lived decisions are higher in the continental tradition.

COMMON LAW AND STATUTES

Formal rules may change spontaneously (i.e., endogenous changes) in order to adjust the prevailing institutions to new requirements of the game, or they can be imposed from without (i.e., exogenous changes) in order to force the game to adjust to new rules. Common law rules are a major vehicle for making *endogenous rules*. The legislative process is a major method for exogenous changes in formal rules.

---

[1] R. Posner, *Economic Analysis of Law*, pp. 539-40. Posner suggests that the rate of depreciation of precedents in the United States is about 4-5 percent.

Legislation

The legislative process is directly influenced by the people who expect to be affected by proposed legislation. Suppose 100 people in a community support a rule that allows a factory to emit smoke. They expect the rule to be worth $100 to each of them individually. The cost of that rule is borne by all members of the community, say 2,000 people, including the 100 beneficiaries. The expected cost of the rule per person is $7. It would be easy to assert that the rule is inefficient because the total cost of allowing the factory to emit smoke is $14,000 while the total benefits are $10,000. The assertion could be wrong. In a world of uncertainty and incomplete knowledge, the basis for individual choices is not perfect foresight but the perception of the future consequences of current decisions. Current expectations and future results are likely to differ, and it is quite possible that the decision allowing the factory to emit smoke might turn out to be an efficient one.

Given their perception of expected benefits, 100 individuals have incentives to invest up to $93 in convincing legislators that the rule allowing factories to emit smoke should be passed. Other members of the community have incentives to invest only up to $7 per person to prevent the rule from being enacted. The example is hypothetical but plausible. The expected beneficiaries are a small group with high individual stakes in the rule. Their costs of forming an interest group are positive but low relative to potential benefits. The losers are a large group with low individual stakes in blocking the rule. Their costs of organizing a pressure group are high relative to potential benefits.

The legislative process in the case above (1) provides incentives for those who expect to benefits from legislative decisions to invest resources in seeking favorable outcomes, and (2) weakens the credibility of the prevailing rules of the game. The process does not provide legislators with incentives to block rules that are expected to waste resources.

Moreover, the legislative process creates incentives favoring rules that are expected to be inefficient. Legislators have a valuable property right, namely the power to confer the gains and to impose the costs on individuals. The legislative process, then, creates a market in which legislators could sell (or block) a redistribution of wealth in exchange for support and campaign contributions. It is predictable that individuals, organized groups and business establishments will try to influence public policy by making campaign contributions to specific legislators, paying high lecture fees, and providing them with a variety of other nonpecuniary benefits.

An implication is that the problem is not interest groups but the ability of the state to use political power to reward some and penalize others. George Stigler wrote:

> The state is a potential resource or threat to every industry in the society. With its power to prohibit or compel, to take or give money, the state can and does selectively help or hurt a vast number of industries.[1]

Analysis in this section does not say that legislators are crooks; it merely says that legislators like all other individuals respond to incentives. Analysis does not dispute the fact that many legislators have sponsored formal rules that have meant to be beneficial; it says that in a world of uncertainty and imperfect knowledge ex ante intentions and ex post outcome do not necessarily coincide. Analysis does not rule out that rules pushed through legislature by various pressure groups might turn out to be beneficial. All that analysis in this section says is that the process under which legislators work does not have a built-in bias to seek and sustain efficient rules.

Common Law

Common law judges, like all other people, prefer more satisfaction to less satisfaction. Do the prevailing incentives structures under which they work have an efficiency bias? The answer is a weak yes, for three reasons.

First, common law judges are under competitive pressure to seek efficient precedents. Inefficient precedents would result in replacement of courts with private arbitrations and out-of-court agreements. Second, legislators deal directly with individuals and groups, while common law judges deal primarily with activities. This is especially true of judges in the appellate courts, where most

---

[1] G. Stigler, "The Theory of Government Regulation," *Bell Journal of Economics* 2 (1971), p. 3.

precedents are made. By making it difficult for common law judges to seek a monetary payoff, the rules of the judicial process reduce the influence of various pressure groups. Finally, major sources of utility for common law judges are nonmonetary goods, such as power, prestige, and leisure. They make judges sensitive to being reversed by higher courts and eager to contribute to new precedents. Posner notes:

> An odd feature of [the production of precedents] is that the producers are not paid. Neither the judges nor the lawyers in Hadley vs. Baxendale received any royalties or other compensation for a precedent that has guided the decision of thousands of cases....The costs to judges of professional criticism are modest, but because the rules of judicial tenure and compensation attenuate the usual incentives that operate on people, judges are likely to be influenced by what in most walks of life is a weak force.[1]

The system, then, provides incentives for common law judges to conform to the prevailing mode of thinking about social and economic issues, to have a conservative bias in judging disputes in their courts, and to attempt to create precedents when they believe that those precedents have a chance to last. As old precedents are dropped and new ones are added to the legal system, judge-made decisions are marginal adjustments of the prevailing set of formal rules to changes in the game. Formal rules that emerge from within the system are then likely to be in tune with the prevailing informal institutions in the community. That is, those formal rules create incentives to reduce the transaction costs of maintaining and enforcing the prevailing institutional framework. Buchanan wrote:

> The object of the never-ending search by loosely coordinated judges acting independently is to find "the law", to locate and redefine the structure of individual rights, not ab initio, but in existing social-institutional arrangements... Law is a stabilizing influence which provides the necessary framework within which individuals can plan their own affairs.[2]

---

[1] R. Posner, *Economic Analysis of Law*, p. 541.
[2] J. Buchanan, *Freedom in Constitutional Contract* (College Station: Texas A&M University Press, 1975), pp. 46-7.

An implication of this analysis is that common law does have a tendency, and no more than a tendency, to seek and sustain efficient rules.

FORMAL AND INFORMAL RULES, TRANSACTION COSTS, AND ECONOMIC PERFORMANCE[*]

The prevailing institutional framework in a society consists of formal and informal rules, all of which carry their own incentives and transaction costs. Formal rules are externally enforced. The enforcement of informal rules is internalized into the benefits and costs of specific activities. Those costs could range from loss of reputation to rejection by the community.

Clearly, informal rules are not a policy variable, while formal rules are. This means that by freeing resources for alternative uses, formal rules that have lower transaction costs contribute more to the production of wealth than do those with higher transaction costs. Institutional changes and the production of wealth are then linked *via* the effects of the former on transaction costs.

The effects of a change in formal rules depends on the response of informal institutions to that change. If and when formal rules are in tune with informal rules, the incentives both create will tend to reinforce each other. A harmonious interaction of formal and informal rules reduces the transaction costs of maintaining and protecting the rules of the game, and frees some resources for the production of wealth.

However, when formal rules are in conflict with informal rules, their respective incentives will tend to raise the transaction costs of maintaining and enforcing the prevailing institutional environment, and to reduce the production of wealth in the community. The choice of new formal rules is then a major circumstance affecting incentives to lower or raise transaction costs. This means that the incentive structures under which rule makers work and the prevailing constraints on their power to pursue their own private ends determine their

---

[*] This section is reprinted with permission from S. Pejovich, "Law, Tradition, and the Transition in Eastern Europe," *The Independent Review: A Journal of Political Economy*, 2, No 2 (1997).Copyright 1997. The Independent Institute, 134 Ninety-Eighth Avenue, Oakland, CA 94603.

opportunity sets as well as the trade-offs in the process of changing rules.

Examples of the effects of the interaction of formal and informal rules on human behavior are many, and varied. Those examples help us to learn more about the consequences of alternative institutional structures.

The formal rule that limited the maximum speed on American highways to 55 miles per hour was clearly in conflict with the driving culture of most American motorists and raised enforcement costs. Prohibition laws in the United States were clearly in conflict with the country's prevailing tradition of social drinking. The Al Capones served the important social function of giving people what they wanted, at a price. Eventually, the high transaction costs of maintaining and enforcing prohibition laws convinced the government to eliminate the conflict between formal and informal rules concerning the consumption of liquor. That is, people who went to jail for selling liquor in one year were contributing to the country's GNP the following year.

The interaction of formal and informal rules explains the costs of resources that were required to maintain and enforce the old regimes in Eastern Europe. It explains the differences in economic development between Catholic and Protestant countries in Europe, and the differences in the costs of enforcing the right to life in religious and less religious communities. The rise of "ghettos" in American cities reflected a tendency on the part of various ethnic, racial, and religious groups (all those groups lived under the same set of formal rules) to stay together with those individuals whose behavior they could predict.

North observed that similar formal rules tend to produce different results under different circumstances:

> The US Constitution was adopted with modifications by many Latin American countries in the nineteenth century, and many of the property rights laws of successful Western countries have been adopted by third world countries. The results are, however, not similar to those in the United States or other successful Western countries. The enforcement mechanism, the

norms of behavior, and the subjective models of the actors are not [the same].[1]

It is difficult to develop a method for evaluating the effects of the interaction of formal and informal rules on transactions costs. A promising approach is as follows: Suppose the leaders of a country decide to make a major change in that country's formal institutions, such as President Lyndon Johnson's Civil Rights Bill in 1964. A new rule signals the rulers' intention of restructuring the prevailing formal institutions. However, basic laws are always either too general or too ambiguous to have much immediate operational impact. This means that the new rule has to be integrated into the prevailing system of formal and informal institutions. To do that, public policy makers have to pass clarifying rules and regulations. I conjecture that the number of those secondary regulations depends on the reaction of the prevailing informal rules to the new formal rule.

Secondary laws and regulations are costly. First, they consume current wealth. Second, they also reduce the production of wealth in the future by creating a perception of frequent legal changes. Thus, the number as well as the content of clarifying laws and regulation can be taken as a proxy for the effect of the new rule on transaction costs.

Thrainn Eggertsson summarized the interaction thesis as follows:

> The basic idea underlying the [interaction thesis] is that formal rules interact with informal rules (culture) and outcomes will differ from the nominal implications of formal rules, if the two are inconsistent in some sense. The viewpoint suggests that attempts to introduce structural change from above must be consistent with people's informal mental models, if they are to be successful. Furthermore, different cultures are likely to follow different approaches to decentralized exchange systems, and it is hard to predict which path will be taken in a process that involves evolution and learning.

---

[1] D North, *Institutions, Institutional Change and Economic Performance*, p. 101.

LAW AND THE TRANSITION PROCESS IN EASTERN EUROPE

It is clear that in 1989, East Europeans wanted socialist rule to end. By mid-1990, pro-collectivist parties (communists, socialists, fascists) were doing well in free elections. The purpose of this section is to show that the transition process based on exogenous institutional changes is a major reason for the rising strength of those parties.

For several decades East Europeans were forced to live under a system that tolerated neither the free market for ideas nor contacts with the rest of the world.[1] As socialist rule ended, East Europeans were in no position to identify quickly alternative institutional arrangements and/or evaluate their expected consequences. There is evidence, however, that ordinary people in Eastern Europe were in favor of capitalism as they perceived the system. After several decades (seven in the former USSR) of Marxist indoctrination, East Europeans did not and could not see capitalism as a way of life in which each and every individual bears the value consequences of his or her decisions. The prevailing perception of capitalism was to identify it with bountiful supplies of goods and equally large incomes to buy those goods. The benefits of capitalism were somehow to be captured with neither a change in work ethic nor a reduction in the prevailing welfare programs. The transition process quickly disillusioned people about the system as they perceived it.

At the same time many of us in the West interpreted the end of socialism in Eastern Europe to be a vote for capitalism as we understand the system. Thus, we encouraged new leaders in Eastern Europe to use the strong hand of the state to "build" capitalism in their respective countries. From the standpoint of ordinary people in Eastern Europe, the transition process then became a substitution of one set of institutions for another set, neither of which they chose for themselves.

---

[1] Yugoslavia was the only exception.

Formal and Informal Rules in Eastern Europe

Socialist rule in Eastern Europe subverted the rule of law to the will of the ruling elite and seriously undermined people's confidence in enforcement mechanisms. During the immediate post-1989 period, the prevailing socialist institutions have been destabilized. Perceiving an institutional vacuum, East Europeans needed a stable set of rules for carrying out transactions among themselves and with the rest of the world. And they began to fall back on their *informal* norms of behavior. With its emphasis on ethnicity, the extended family, and shared values, the old ethos was a powerful fortress; behind its walls most people had been able to hide and learn to live with socialist institutions without ever accepting them. An unintended effect of socialist rule, then, was to preserve the region's informal rules.

The behavior fostered by this tradition is, however, limited to a group of people who share the same traditions and values. For example, the rise of "ghettos" in many large American cities reflects a tendency on the part of ethnic, racial and religious groups to stay around those whose behavior they can predict. Street riots, zoning issues, civil disturbances and various forms of real or, more likely, perceived discrimination are predictable consequences of interactions between mutual aliens. In Eastern Europe, people who share the same tradition are usually members of the same ethnic group. Interactions within any specific group are thus subject to rules of behavior that do not necessarily hold in exchanges across ethnic lines. The Serbs in Croatia, the Albanians in Serbia, the Turks in Bulgaria, and the Hungarians in Romania are examples of ethnic groups seeking cultural autonomy.

Evidence is plentiful that the old ethos has affected the behavior of ordinary people toward capitalism in the transition process. They see the gains from exchange as a redistribution of wealth rather than as rewards that individuals receive for creating new value. State authorities are more likely to shutdown operators who earn large profits by producing and/or selling goods for which supplies are low relative to demand than to encourage others to emulate such individuals in open markets. Members of collective farms in Russia are making life difficult for farmers who choose to go private. Small shop owners in the Ukraine are treated as second class citizens. There is also a common conviction in Eastern Europe that resources are found rather than created. Thus, the accumulation of private wealth in many East European communities is suspect.

It is true that capitalism had to face similar problems in many other countries with strong collectivist traditions. Chile, Japan, South Korea and Taiwan, among other countries, have given their people opportunities to experiment with alternative institutional arrangements. People responded by exploiting various opportunities and adopted those that passed the market test. Eventually, most of those countries ended up with a blend of capitalist institutions and old traditions. On the other hand, new leaders in Eastern Europe, with considerable support from the West, used the strong hand of the state to "give" capitalism to their people. And they have, except in a few countries, failed. An implication is that the method of choosing institutions matters.

Former Nomenklaturists and the Transition Process

As socialist rule ended in Eastern Europe, former leaders had incentives to seek ways to preserve their power and privileges. Their human capital qualified them for seeking advantages in a bureaucratic environment; therefore, a free-market, private-property system was a threat to their private well-being. To preserve the value of their human capital, former communists, while paying lip service to free- market reforms, somehow had to create a state-centered system. They realized that encouraging the perception of an external threat to their respective ethnic groups would give them their best chance to create such a system. Most former communists, then, quickly transformed themselves into nationalists. It was an easy thing for them to do because nationalism and socialism have one important common trait: the collectivist mode of looking at the world.

In general, nationalism represents the conviction that the community's common good transcends the private ends of its members. This implies that individuals can attain their greatest potential only through their nationality. Nationalism is thus incompatible with individual liberty and competitive markets. Indeed, most leaders in the multiethnic states of Eastern Europe in the early 1990s were nonreformed communists such as Milosevic in Serbia, Kucan in Slovenia, Meciar in Slovakia and Kravchuk in the Ukraine. The case of Czechoslovakia in the early 1990s is good evidence. In their quest to retain power, former communists in Slovakia adroitly exploited Slovak nationalism, eventually separating the country into two sovereign states. In contrast, the Czechs, with virtually no former communists in positions of power, are treating ethnic issues as a nuisance that could only interfere with getting the country on the road to economic recovery.

It is important not to confuse patriotism with nationalism. Patriotism means attachment to a community and its tradition. However, it is compatible with a voluntary association of diverse individuals who choose to live together. Unlike nationalism, patriotism is consistent with individual liberty, pursuit of private ends, and cultural diversity.

Older Workers and the Transition Process

East Europeans had no opportunity to save and invest in "owned" assets during socialist rule. Instead, the state provided them with assets *specific* to a non-private property economy. Those assets consisted of (i) a variety of welfare benefits such as job security, allowances for children, medical benefits, and subsidized housing; and (ii) the shortage economy.

Retired people and older workers (forty-five plus) find the returns from those assets irreplaceable. Hence they have incentives to oppose the transition from socialism to capitalism. Older workers see capitalism as a threat to their current and future benefits from the system-specific assets. They fear, and for good reason, that the reminder of their working life is not long enough to allow them to replace those benefits with private saving and investments. Retired people have already seen a decline in the value of their pensions and other benefits. In addition, the shortage economy made them an important asset to their families in two ways. First, they had time to wait in line for consumer goods. Second, they specialized in knowing what goods would be available, and where and when they were going to be available. Thus, they raised the real incomes of their families. As scarcity prices replace price controls, retired people fear that they will become a liability to their families.

Predictably, older workers and retirees perceive the transition from socialism to capitalism as a real threat to the value of their assets accumulated during socialist rule. They didn't purchase those assets by choice but that is all they got. Thus, a major segment of the population in Eastern Europe is hostile to capitalism for reasons of self-interest, whatever their ideological preference might be. Evidence is consistent with this proposition. Young people, who have made no investment in the old system's specific assets, are strong supporters of a transition to capitalism, while older workers and retired people tend to support pro-collectivist parties.

Implications of The Transition Process

A major characteristic of most transition models is that they endorse institutional changes, such as privatization of state factories[1] and the methods for organizing production,[2] that have to be introduced by fiat. Most state factories in Eastern Europe have no chance to survive in competitive markets. Yet, we already observe that ordinary people fail to attribute dismal performance of those firms to the decades of communist mismanagement. Instead, they tend to say: "The free-market, private-property economy is not working either."

Some spontaneous institutional changes have occurred in Eastern Europe. For example, private-ownership firms have emerged in most countries even though private property rights are yet to enjoy credible legal guarantees. However, exogenous institutional changes have dominated the transition from socialism to capitalism. What are some specific and predictable effects of exogenous changes on preferences of the median voter in Eastern Europe?

1. *Exogenous changes require an activist government as a means of imposing and maintaining them.* In Eastern Europe, the role of the strong hand of the state in the transition process is usually justified by reference to either the "public interest" or the efficiency- enhancing

---

[1] Most state factories in Eastern Europe have no chance to survive in competitive markets. Yet, we already observe that ordinary people fail to attribute dismal performance of those firms to the decades of communist mismanagement. Instead, they tend to say: "The free-market, private-property economy is not working either."

[2] For detailed analysis of the effects of exogenous changes on the choice of business enterprises see Pejovich, S. "A Property Rights Analysis of Alternative Methods of Organizing Production," *Communist Economies and Economic Transformation* 6, No. 2, (1994).

consequences of capitalist institutions. Both justifications are misleading.

The public interest argument assumes that the social welfare function exists and that public decision makers (could) know it. Neither assumption is derivable from scientific knowledge. An attempt to justify exogenous changes by reference to the maximization paradigm of neoclassical economics conveys a message that capitalism is a "mechanism" for the allocation of resources, which, by implication, may or may not outperform alternative institutional arrangements. It is a bad message because the critical difference between capitalism and alternative arrangements, including socialism, is not in their quantitative performance but in their respective impacts on the way of life in society.

2. *Another consequence of exogenous changes is a contraction in the social opportunity set.*[1] Two factors are responsible for this outcome. First, exogenous changes interfere with "the constraints that are voluntarily arrived at when individuals are free to impose restrictions upon themselves."[2] Second, in a world of uncertainty and incomplete knowledge, social engineers and public decision makers do not and cannot possess reliable information about the economy's dynamic responses to exogenous institutional changes. Human interactions continuously create and disseminate new knowledge. The assimilation and interpretation of this knowledge by different individuals keeps changing opportunity sets and expectations about future. To assume that individuals' utility functions are **a** given is thus misleading. They are continuously modified by the action-choosing process.

A dissipation of resources is then a predictable consequence of exogenous changes. In many East European countries, the effects of exogenous changes on the social opportunity set have revealed themselves via inflation and unemployment.

---

[1] The social opportunity set is not confined to standard goods and services. It also includes all socioeconomic and sociopolitical institutions. See Jensen, M. and Meckling, W. "Rights and Production Functions: An Application to Labor-Managed Firms and Codetermination," *Journal of Business* 52, No 4, (1979), pp. 470-2.
[2] Alchian, A. and Woodward, S. "The Firm is Dead; Long Live the Firm," *Journal of Economic Literature* 26, (1988), p. 65.

3. *Finally, the people who impose exogenous changes and those who implement them are not the same people.* The latter have considerable discretionary power in interpreting the intent of policy makers. They also have their own incentives and private ends that are likely to differ from those of their superiors. A predictable outcome in Eastern Europe has been a difference between the promised and observed results of the transition process.

Conclusions

The transition process "imposed" some institutions of capitalism in Eastern Europe with little regard for the region's philosophical heritage, the way East Europeans perceived capitalism before 1989, the importance that well-defined groups attach to assets specific to the old system, or the role of local leaders in exploiting nationalism. Because they identify the results of the transition process with capitalism, East Europeans are voting free-market parties out of power.

An alternative approach to institutional changes in Eastern Europe is to let people choose their way of life. Spontaneous institutional changes cannot and would not guarantee that East Europeans will choose capitalism. However, the market for institutions would give them a chance to identify alternative arrangements, try them out, adjust to their consequences, and select those they prefer.

Indeed, we already observe thousands of small private firms--mostly kiosks and miniature shops--which have spontaneously emerged throughout Eastern Europe in spite of the absence of credible legal guarantees of private property rights. Many of those shops will not last but some will grow. While their economic significance is still modest, such private enterprises are the breeding ground for entrepreneurs, a work ethic, a capitalist exchange culture, and positive attitudes toward capitalism in general. They educate ordinary people to appreciate a way of life that rewards performance, promotes individual liberties, and places high value on self-responsibility and self-determination.

SUGGESTED READING

Cukierman, A. and Meltzer, A. "A Positive Theory of Discretionary Policy, the Cost of Democratic Government and the Benefits of a Constitution," Economic Inquiry 24, 1986.

Chapter 5

PROPERTY RIGHTS

Property rights are relations among individuals that arise from the existence of scarce goods and pertain to their use. They are the norms of behavior that individuals must observe in interaction with others or bear the costs of violation. Property rights do not define the relationship between individuals and objects. Instead, they define the relationship among individuals with respect to all scarce goods. The prevailing institutions are the aggregation of property rights that individuals have.

My right to vote defines my position vis-à-vis other members of the community with respect to the choice of government. My right to a computer in my office defines my position vis-à-vis other individuals with respect to the access to that computer. Both rights are property rights.

Roman law provided the enduring legal and philosophical foundations for property rights, and developed a number of well-defined categories of property rights that have survived the test of time. This chapter discusses three major types of property rights: private property rights, communal property, and state or public property. The book also makes use of some other categories of property rights such as usus fructus (the right to use a scarce good belonging to someone else or to rent it to others, but not to sell it or change its substance), and usus (the right to use a scarce good belonging to someone else, but not to rent it or sell it or change its substance).

Private Property Rights

Writing on the concept of private property rights, Irwin Fisher said:

> A property right is a liberty or permit to enjoy benefits of wealth--in its broadest sense--while assuming the costs which those benefits entail...It will be observed that property rights,

unlike wealth or benefits, are not physical objects nor events, but are abstract social relations. A property right is not a thing.[1]

The right of ownership contains three elements: exclusivity of ownership, transferability of ownership, and constitutional guarantees of ownership. Those three elements of private property rights have predictable effects on economic behavior.

Exclusivity of Ownership

The exclusivity of ownership means that the owner has the right to choose what to do with an asset (e.g., the right to speak on a social issue), how to use it (e.g., to oppose abortion), and who is to be given access to it (e.g., to authorize an anti abortion league to speak for the owner). The owner decides what to do with the assets, captures the benefits of the decision, and bears its cost. The exclusivity of ownership then creates a strong link between one's right to choose how to use assets and bearing the consequences of that choice.

The right of ownership is not an unrestricted right. But it is limited only by restrictions explicitly stated in the law. We observe attenuation of the right of ownership in scarce goods that range from substantial ones, such as price controls, to minor restrictions, such as keeping the fence around one's house two feet inside the property line. By reducing the owner's set of choices, attenuation of private property rights in a good lowers its value to the owner.

Internalizing the costs of using (or not using) a resource means that the right of ownership creates strong incentives for the owner of an asset to seek the best use for that asset. The world is full of observations that support this proposition. People take better care of homes they own than of those they rent. They are more likely to add oil to cars they own than to those they rent. I have two computers. The computer at home is mine while the one in the office belongs to the university. They render the same flow of services to me, yet I do not value them equally. I have more rights in the home, the car, and the computer that is mine.

---

[1] Fisher, I. Elementary Principles of Economics, (New York: Macmillan, 1923), p. 27.

Transferability of Ownership

The transferability of ownership means that the owner has the right to transfer an asset to others at mutually agreed upon terms. It provides individuals with a choice that other types of property rights do not. The choice is to take the value of their assets in a lump sum or as a flow over the life of their respective assets. An important consequence of this choice is that each and every person can rearrange her portfolio in accordance with both her subjective perceptions of what the future holds as well as the attitude toward risk. Moreover, the transferability of assets provides incentives for resources to move from less optimistic to more optimistic owners.

Suppose Ms. Smith is a farmer. Working her farm as best as she knows how, Ms. Smith makes about $1,000 per year after all expenses including her opportunity costs. Ms. Jones believes she could earn $1,500 over her opportunity costs farming the same land. That is, she believes she could produce a larger output. A transfer of the farm from Ms. Smith to Ms. Jones would maximize the value of production if Ms Jones' optimism turns out to be appropriate.

The transferability of ownership provides incentives for the farm to be transferred to Ms. Jones. Assuming an interest rate of 10 percent, Ms. Jones would be willing to pay up to $15,000 for the farm, while Ms. Smith would have incentives to sell the farm at any price above $10,000. If Ms. Smith's subjective evaluation of the value of her farm exceeds $15,000, she would bear the entire cost of her decision not to sell the farm. If Ms. Jones optimism turns out to be unwarranted, she would bear the costs of her investment.

Some scholars have questioned the proposition that the transferability of private property rights moves resources to their highest-valued uses.[1] What they seem to be questioning is the maximization paradigm of the standard neoclassical model. The theory of property rights does not say that resources go to the highest-valued user. The theory merely says that private property rights create more

---

[1] See B. Larson, and D. Bromley, "Property Rights, Externalities, and Resource Degradation: Locating the Tragedy," *Journal of Development Economics* 33 (1990), pp. 235-262; and L. Putterman, "Markets, Hierarchies, and Information: On a Paradox in the Economic Organization," *Journal of Economic Behavior and Organization* 26 (1995), pp. 373-390.

incentives for individuals to reduce transaction costs of exchange, to seek new opportunities for exchange, and to enter in exchange agreements that are expected to be beneficial than do all other types of property rights. Those incentives of private property rights are observable and consistent with a tendency to seek efficient outcomes.

The Constitutional Guarantee of Ownership

By protecting private property rights from the rule of the majority and/or the ruling elite, the constitutional guarantee of ownership divorces economic wealth from political power. In a non-private property society, one's economic well-being improves as one moves up the power structure. If and when a person gets kicked out of the power structure that individual loses all economic benefits.

Quite a few people in the socialist world have gone straight from a relative affluence to a gulag. And nomenklaturists who were lucky to avoid a camp did not escape economic poverty and social ostracism. On the capitalist side of the fence, when President Richard Nixon resigned from the White House, he kept his wealth. In capitalism, the constitutionality of ownership breaks the link between political power and economic wealth. The individual who loses political power does not lose economic wealth.

Political power is not the exclusive road to wealth in socialism (for example, athletes and artists did well in the former USSR); and the separation of power from wealth is far from perfect in capitalism. But, in general, a major consequence of the absence of private property rights is the marriage of political power and wealth, and a major consequence of the right of ownership is their divorce. By protecting economic wealth from political power, the constitutional guarantee of ownership creates incentives for individuals to make long-lived investment decisions.

To summarize the effects of the three major elements of the right of ownership: Exclusivity provides incentives for owners to put their assets into the best uses they are capable of discovering; transferability provides incentives for resources to move from less optimistic to more optimistic individuals; that is, to those individuals who believe that they could do better with the same bundle of resources; and the constitutional guarantee of ownership separates the accumulation of economic wealth from the accumulation of political power. In a world of uncertainty and incomplete knowledge, private property rights then provide a strong tendency for the resources to move in the direction of greater efficiency.

State Ownership

The term *state ownership* is merely a facade hiding the true owner, which is the political elite. State ownership is often called public or social ownership; those terms are used interchangeably. We observe many examples of public ownership in the United States, such as Hoover Dam, the Tennessee Valley Authority, national parks, and military bases. Members of the political elite have the right to choose how to use state-owned resources, the right to allocate the flow of pecuniary and nonpecuniary income from those resources, and the right to control who has what access to those benefits.

The cost of the goods produced by state-owned resources is the value of output that is forgone. With a few exceptions, those goods are sold below their costs. When we visit Yellowstone National Park, the entrance fee does not cover the cost of services we receive; that is, private costs we incur are below the social costs of running the park. The total social cost is spread over all taxpayers, including those who never visit the park. On the other hand, when we visit Disneyland, the price we pay has to be sufficient to cover the costs of running the place; that is, private costs approach social costs. A consequence of state ownership is thus the presence of externality; those who consume the good do not bear the entire costs of their consumption.

Public decision makers do not capture the benefits of their decisions, either. No matter what the state agency charges for its product, neither its officers nor their superiors can appropriate the residual after cooperating inputs (i.e., employees) are paid their contractual prices.

Public decision makers, then, have weak incentives to invest time and resources in identifying the highest-valued uses for state-owned goods they control, and strong incentives to invest time and resources seeking beneficial trade-offs (pecuniary as well as nonpecuniary) for themselves. An implication is that public decision makers' subjective perceptions of political reality explain the allocation of state-owned resources. That is, inefficiencies in government have less to do with the professionalism, work habits and integrity of public decision makers than with the penalty/reward system arising from state ownership in scarce goods.

Table 5-1 compares the expected effects of those incentives by reference to the use of a tree in private and state-owned forests. The table ignores the consequences of changes in the value of land on which the tree is planted. Data in the example are hypothetical.

The table shows the returns from investing $100 in a live tree. The owner bears the cost in a private forest, while taxpayers pay for the tree in a public forest. From one year to another, the amount of lumber in the live tree increases. For convenience, we assume that the amount of lumber increases at a decreasing rate from the very first year. Column 2 shows the value of lumber in the live tree at the end of each year, in constant prices. Like all resources, the tree has alternative uses. We can cut it and use the lumber to make homes. Or we can invest the proceeds from the sale of lumber. It is important to understand that cutting the tree does not destroy a resource but merely changes its use.

At the end of each year, the owner has a choice of either keeping the tree alive or cutting it, selling the lumber, and reinvesting the proceeds at the going rate of interest, say 15 percent. Driven by self-interest, the owner has incentives to keep the tree alive for as long as the rate of growth in the value of lumber in the live tree exceeds the rate of interest. For example, at the end of the third year the owner can cut the tree, sell the lumber for $304, and invest that money at the going rate of 15 percent. In a year, that investment would grow from $304 to $350. The alternative of not cutting the tree is clearly preferable. In one year, the owner expects the value of lumber in the live tree to increase to $411. The right of ownership provides strong incentives not to cut the tree at the end of the third year.

If the owner needed money to send a daughter to college he could sell the tree for at least $304. And the new owner would have incentives to let the tree grow. When the rate of growth in the expected value of lumber in the live tree approximates the rate of interest (year eight in our example), the owner would have incentives to cut the tree or sell to a more optimistic owner (one who expects interest rates to fall, or the price of lumber to increase, or both). Cutting the tree down at the end of year eight converts the live tree into a more valuable form of wealth. From the standpoint of the community, the right of ownership provides incentives for the owner to bear the cost of discovering the most efficient time to cut the tree.

Table 5-1. The Value of Lumber in a Live Tree

Year	Value of Lumber in Dollars	Rate of Growth as %
1	150	50
2	217	45
3	304	40
4	411	35
5	534	30
6	668	25
7	801	20
8	922	15
9	1,024	10
10	1,065	5

When the tree is owned by the state, the decision maker in charge of running public forests may cut the tree at the end of year eight. Since the costs and benefits of cutting the tree are dissipated throughout the economy, neither that decision maker nor more senior superiors have incentives to relate the rate of growth in the value of lumber in the live tree to the going rate of interest. Hence economic analysis cannot predict whether the tree is going to be cut in that year. It really depends on the decision maker's (or superior's) private ends. And public decision makers can choose to pursue their private ends because the costs and benefits of their choices are borne by others. There are examples of forests that have been devastated to provide governments with cash. There are also many examples in which trees have not been cut because the government was influenced by those who consider conservation of wildlife a superior good. In the United States, Vice President Al Gore in the 1990s and former Secretary of Interior James Watt in the 1980s had different preferences regarding the best use of public forests.

Conservationists frequently ask for governmental controls over the use of specific resources. Their argument rests on two points: They assert that the actual rate of consumption of those resources is too high and should be reduced, and they claim that many people have wrong ideas about the most valuable use for those resources. As

Armen Alchian likes to say, such an argument is simply an assertion that certain people should not have their preferences satisfied.

Communal Ownership

Communal ownership means that a well-defined group of people jointly hold a nontransferable asset. Ordinarily, members of the group have the right to decide how to use the asset and the right to allocate proceeds. But *they have no right to sell those two rights to others.* Otherwise, communal ownership would be no different from private ownership. Even if the right to sell one's share of communal property were restricted, it would be more correct to define that property right as an attenuated ownership.

In general, the rights are acquired by joining the group and lost by leaving it. In tribal communities, communal ownership in land was and is quite frequent. In modern times, we observe a great variety of types of communal ownership, including producers' cooperatives and labor-managed firms. Communal ownership has three important consequences.

First, consider a group of 100 people who have the right to graze their cows on a pasture held in common. Each member of the group has a herd of 20 cows worth $100 per head. Given the amount of grass available on the pasture, grazing an additional cow would result in less weight per cow. And the price per cow would fall to $99. Suppose a member of the group decides to add a cow to *his* herd. The value of his herd would increase by $79, while the total value of all the cows owned by the other 99 group members would decline from $198,000 to $196,020. A decision by a group member to increase his herd by one cow shifts some of the costs to others. Communal ownership then creates incentives for members of the group to overutilize assets that are held in common.

Second, an individual captures a share of the benefits from resources held in common only through membership in the group. In a world of uncertainty and incomplete knowledge, individuals cannot be sure of how long they will remain members of the group. Hence communal ownership creates incentives for the group to use a high discount rate in evaluating long-lived investments.

Third, each and every member of the group has incentives to shirk. Transaction costs of preventing (or reducing) shirking depend on the group's size and the nature of its asset.

We observe many forms of communal ownership in the world we live in, such as communal ownership in land, country clubs, condominiums, producers' and consumers' cooperatives, and labor-managed firms. Some kinds of communal ownership receive legal protection, subsidies, or tax incentives from the state. The fact that they have to get support from the state is evidence of their inefficiency.

However, we also observe many types of communal ownership based on voluntary contracts. Communal ownership tends to replace private property rights when two conditions exist: (1) the owner's costs of excluding others from access to a good are relatively high, and (2) the costs of monitoring the behavior of members of the group are relatively low.

The development of property rights in many Swiss villages is a good example. Individual farmers have private property right in their land, homes, cattle, etc. However, pastures on the hillside above the village are usually held in common by the villagers. If the hillside were parceled out among villagers, transaction costs of keeping cows belonging to one farmer from grazing on the land of another would be high. At the same time, transaction costs to the villagers as a group of excluding non-villagers from grazing their herds on the hillside are low. A number of informal rules have emerged to reduce transaction costs of monitoring the use of the hillside pastures by villagers. For example, in some villages, rights to pastures held in common are allocated according to the number of cows that individual farmers could feed during the winter with hay produced on their respective farms.[1]

THE DEVELOPMENT OF PROPERTY RIGHTS

Let us begin with goods that are free for all. In general, a good is free for all when the costs of establishing, policing and enforcing a right in that good are high relative to the perceived benefits from that right. Sometimes, the government decides that some goods, such as a public

---

[1] E. Ostrom, "Private and Common Property Rights," Working paper, Workshop in Political Theory and Policy Analysis, Indiana University, 1996, p. 14.

beach, are to be free in order to assure access to that beach for all citizens. Whatever its political merits might be, the open-access argument confuses the free access to a good with the creation of wealth. If the beach were privately owned, any individual or group willing to pay the opportunity costs of that land would have free access to the beach. However, keeping the beach free for all eliminates incentives for that asset to move from those who value it but value it less to those who value it more.

The rationing criterion for a free-for-all good is first come, first served. If I choose not to cut a beautiful young tree in a free-for-all forest, someone else will. My cost of purchasing that tree is the value of my time plus the (prorated) value of the tools I need to use to cut the tree. I do not have to pay the market price of the live tree. Externality is present because the private costs of acquiring the tree are lower than its social costs. The rate of consumption of free-for-all goods should thus be expected to exceed the rate that would prevail if some kind of property rights in those goods were established and enforced.

The rate of investment in a free-for-all good is also affected. The investor has to bear the entire cost of policing and enforcing future benefits; perhaps even be willing and able to use violence to exclude all competitors. The rate of investment in free-for-all assets should then be expected to fall short of what the rate of investment would be if some kind of property rights in those assets were established and enforced.

Empirical evidence supports both propositions. One might ask why fishing, golfing and swimming are better at private lakes, private clubs and private beaches than at public lakes, municipal golf courses, and free-for-all beaches? One might also wonder what happened to the buffalo, the whale, publicly owned forests, and many rivers? If one is to blame human greed for the destruction of those resources, then why have the same presumably greedy humans preserved cattle, the fertility of private farms, young trees in privately owned forests, clean water in private lakes, and many other scarce resources?

An implication is that individuals have incentives to exclude others from the free access (i.e., to specify property rights) to a free-for-all good whenever *their* perceived benefits exceed *their* cost of policing and enforcing the claim. And to exclude others from the uncontrolled access to a good means to define property rights in that good. New property rights in a resource are then created and existing ones modified in response to changes in either the perceived benefits from those changes or the cost of defining, policing and enforcing new property rights in that resource. An unintended effect of this spontaneous change in property rights is to internalize some externalities and reduce the difference between private and social costs of using that good.

For example, in the early days of the Roman Empire a form of communal ownership called *ager gentilicius* developed. Agri gentilicii were pastures owned by the Gens (a group of people having a common ancestor), which all members exploited in accordance with their needs. However, as agriculture developed in Rome, the value of crop growing rose relative to that of ranching. Incentives emerged for parceling out the land into smaller units. In time, communal ownership in land broke down into consortiums, a form of nontransferable family ownership in land. Smaller family units captured more rights in their land, some social costs were internalized, and the difference between private and social costs was reduced.

This analysis of the development of property rights suggests a tendency for more efficient property rights to develop spontaneously in response to the interaction between changes in the economic conditions of life and individuals' search for more utility. The role of the authority is a passive one and limited to enforcing new rules of the game.

In a classic paper on the process of change in property rights, Harold Demsetz wrote:

> Before the fur trade became established, hunting was carries out primarily for purpose of food and the relatively few furs that were required for the hunter's family. Externality was clearly present.... But these external effects were of such small significance that it did not pay for anyone to take them into account. There did not exist anything resembling private ownership in land....The advent of fur trade had two immediate consequences. First, the value of furs to the Indians was increased considerably. Second, as a result, the scale of hunting activity rose sharply. Both consequences must have increased considerably the importance of the externalities associated with free hunting. The property right system began to change, and it

changed specifically in the direction required to take account of the economic effects made important by the fur trade.[1]

However, history offers many examples of those in power assuming an active role in changing the prevailing property rights. The effect of exogenous changes in property rights is to force the game to adjust to new rules. While some exogenous changes in property rights might be prudent and justifiable, the problem is the same as with statutes: the ruling elite compels people to accept new rules whether they like them or not. Examples are central planning in the former Soviet Union, the labor-managed economy in the former Yugoslavia, codetermination in Germany, economic growth policies in many Third World countries, and numerous environmental regulations in the United States.

PROPERTY RIGHTS AND ECONOMIC DEVELOPMENT IN ENGLAND AND SPAIN

In medieval Europe, the tradition was for a king to be self-sufficient. He was expected to live (and meet obligations to his subjects) on the income from his land and the traditional feudal taxes. However, changes in military technology, especially the use of gun powder, raised the cost of waging wars. A consequence was that the king needed additional sources of revenue.[2]

To get more revenues, the king had to turn to his subjects and offer protection of property rights in exchange for money. More secure property rights provided incentives to develop new opportunities for exchange and produce more wealth, which the king could then tax. Clearly, a conflict of interest had to arise between crown and constituents with respect to who would get what from the increment in output. The conflict, by creating incentives for a new institution to emerge, led to the development of representative assemblies. The initial purpose of representative assemblies was to represent the constituents in negotiations with the crown.

---

[1] H. Demsetz, "Toward a Theory of Property Rights," *American Economic review* 57 (May 1967), pp. 351-352.

[2] D. North, "Institutions, Economic Growth and Freedom: A Historical Introduction," in *Freedom, Democracy and Economic Welfare*, M. Walker, ed. (Vancouver, B.C.: Fraser Institute, 1988), pp. 14-19. This summary of North's research is mine.

In those negotiations, both sides had incentives to seek the kind of contracts that would enhance their bargaining power. The crown preferred to resolve the conflict of interest with constituents within the prevailing institutional arrangements, which favored medieval guilds and the king's chartered monopolies. The assembly sought to reduce the king's discretionary powers by encouraging the development of new institutions.

At the beginning of the sixteenth century, institutional arrangements in England and Spain were similar and so were their respective levels of economic development. The wool trade was a major source of royal revenues in both countries. However, the relative strength and opportunity costs of the crown and the assembly were not the same. And economic development proceeded along different paths in England and in Spain.

In England, the prevailing statutes covered only existing industries so that new industries were not bound by old rules. Moreover, law enforcement in the countryside was in the hands of judges, who were not paid by the crown. Predictably, new industries moved into the countryside where guilds were much weaker, and price and wage controls were not effectively enforced. The result was the spontaneous development of joint-stock companies and growing resentment against the crown-sponsored monopolies. Eventually, political power shifted from the crown to Parliament. In exchange for the right to set taxes, Parliament guaranteed the king a stable flow of income. Toward the end of the seventeenth century, common law replaced old statutes as the law of the land. By helping to replace statutes with common law, competition among various courts with overlapping jurisdiction contributed to more secure property rights and local political controls. All of that helped to enhance economic growth in England.

In Spain, major sources of the king's revenue were the sheepherders' guild (Mesta), revenues from the empire, and sales tax. In return for the right of sheep owners to move their flocks around the country from one suitable pasture to another, Mesta guaranteed the king a stable flow of income. Consequences of this arrangement were insecure property rights in land and enhanced soil erosion, both of which arrested the development of agriculture. As the balance of power shifted in favor of the crown, the conflict of interest between the crown and its constituents was resolved within the traditional institutional arrangements, and the country's economy declined.

SUGGESTED READING

A. Alchian, *Economic Forces at Work* (Indianapolis: Liberty Press, 1977), Part II.

J. Buchanan, *The Limits of Liberty,* (Chicago: Chicago University Press, 1962).

Chapter 6

CAPITALISM AND SOCIALISM

> The inherent vice of capitalism is the unequal sharing of blessings; the inherent virtue of socialism is the equal sharing of miseries.
>
> Winston Churchill, January 1952

Economic analysis of institutions does not require references to capitalism and socialism. However, it is useful to continue to make this distinction because competition between capitalism and socialism has so dominated the twentieth century. Moreover, the history and development of capitalism and socialism help us understand the forces that contributed to the rise of many institutions. And categorizing some institutions as having the characteristics of capitalism or socialism reduces the cost of identifying their intended consequences.

A few caveats are in order. There has never existed a pure socialist or a pure capitalist country. The preponderance of the institutions of capitalism or socialism in a country determine our perception of that country's system. Analysis here is limited to the institutions that have actually existed and their respective performances. Hence this chapter is not concerned with the institutions of capitalism and socialism that could have existed (that is, blackboard models) nor with the performance that such institutions could have shown.

How did capitalism and socialism emerge? Were they unintended consequences of the gradual evolution of human knowledge and technology, or intended consequences of abstract values and social engineering? Are they predictable outcomes of the laws of history?

THE MIDDLE AGES

The collapse of the Roman Empire eliminated both Roman law, which was based on private ownership and contracts, and the machinery that enforced it. Initially, barbaric customs replaced Roman law as the means of resolving conflicts of interest among competing individuals and groups.

A survival strategy for a weaker man was to turn to a stronger man and give the latter nontransferable right of ownership in his land in exchange for protection and an inalienable right of tenancy--the right to hold the land of the lord. The lord-vassal relationship slowly evolved into a basic social institution in medieval Europe. The land held by the vassal was called the feud. A lord could and often did become the vassal of still another man; that is, he became both the lord of a weaker man and the vassal of a stronger man. Eventually, the high costs of negotiating, policing and enforcing one's rights to life and property in post-Roman Europe gradually led to the development of a socioeconomic system based on a hierarchy of individuals holding specific property rights in land. The king was at the top of this chain, and the actual tillers of the land (serfs) were at the bottom. In comparison with ancient civilizations such as those of India and China, feudalism was a unique system. The uniqueness of the system lay in its pseudo-contractual character. All social classes including the serfs had well-defined rights and obligations, which provided protection from arbitrary decision of kings, princes and bishops.

The Catholic Church (hereafter, the Church) provided a service--the guidance to the attainment of salvation--that customers could neither test before purchase nor learn about the value of from others. Thus, the Church's product had to be a credence good. To secure the credence of its product, the Church needed monopoly in the market for salvation. Its methods for securing monopoly included persecution of heretics, inquisition, threat of damnation, and crusades.

To maintain the credence of its product, the Church also had to guard the revealed doctrine against competing knowledge. Indeed the church acquired a substantial monopoly in the field of education. Libraries were located in monasteries and cathedrals, and the vast majority of literate people were monks. Being the repository of accumulated knowledge, the Church had the power to interpret knowledge, to determine its uses, and to influence the direction of its growth. In a remarkable book on the medieval church, Robert Ekelund and colleagues explain why Galileo had to pay with his life for saying, in the early seventeenth century, that the earth revolves around the sun and that, therefore, the scriptural claim that the earth was the center of the universe was wrong:

Galileo got into trouble because he held the Copernican system to be true and not simply a 'conjecture'. As such, he frontally challenged the veracity of the church in its claim to be the infallible interpreter of infallible Scriptures.... By persecuting Galileo and other high-profile challengers to its doctrinal hegemony, the Church was acting to protect the stream of rents it obtained from being the monopoly provider of supernatural technology.[1]

In order to protect the credence of the Church's product, pope Gregory VII had initiated several measures in the second part of the eleventh century. He declared the supremacy of the papacy over the entire Church; the purpose being to avoid conflicting interpretations of the product. The pope also declared that the clergy must be free from secular control. Finally, he claimed that kings and lords ruled by the grace of God rather than with the consent of their subjects. Thus, the Church had the right to appoint and depose emperors, kings and princes. To enforce those claims, the Church used both the threat of eternal damnation and the exercise of its growing wealth. In a well-researched book on the Middle Ages, William Manchester wrote:

> The entire medieval millennium took on the aspect of triumphant Christendom. As aristocracies arose from the barbaric mire, kings and princes owed their legitimacy to divine authority, and squires became knights by praying all night at Christian altars. Sovereigns courting popularity led crusades to the Holy Land. To eat meat during Lent became a capital offense, sacrilege meant imprisonment, the Church became the wealthiest landowner on the Continent, and the life of every European, from baptism through matrimony to burial, was governed by popes, cardinals.... The clergy, it was believed, would cast decisive votes in determining where each soul would spend the afterlife.[2]

---

[1] R. Ekelund et al., *Sacred Trust: The Medieval Church as an Economic Firm* (Oxford: Oxford University Press, 1996), p. 182.
[2] W. Manchester, *A World Lit Only By Fire* (Boston: Little, Brown and Co. 1993), pp. 9-11.

The rules of the game in the Middle Ages were either determined or approved by the church. Religious life and everyday social life were largely indistinguishable. The role of philosophy was to explain and support theological conclusions. Any conflict between the two was considered to be caused by some philosophical error. Mobility between social classes was limited. People had set places in society with obligations and privileges prescribed for their stations in life. The legitimacy of economic activities was tested by reference to moral teachings of the church, not to utility. And quite importantly, as Galileo found out, the only purpose of knowledge was to enhance understanding of the Church's interpretation of God's intentions in creating the universe.

THE RISE OF CAPITALISM

The established order was strong and resistant to social changes. It would have been impossible for a single factor to bring about institutional restructuring. Institutional restructuring from feudalism to capitalism took several centuries. This section addresses some of the factors that played a role in the great transformation.

The Church as a Rent Seeker

The medieval Church owned a large part of the European economy, and was a residual claimant for much of the rest. The Church was almost the sole source of human capital and a major supplier of capital. The Church therefore had strong incentives to use its monopoly power to engage in rent seeking.

And it did. The Church applied its moral teachings arbitrarily and selectively in order to extract rent. The Church recognized the necessity of trade but warned that trade stimulated the spirit of acquisition, which was perilous to the soul. In practice this meant that it was all right to engage in trade, at a price. The Church condemned the accumulation of wealth in words but tolerated it in practice. Money was considered a nonproductive medium of exchange, and it was morally wrong to charge interest on borrowed funds. Yet, the Church engaged in charging interest on the funds it lent to others as well as maintaining limited financial markets for its own benefits.

An quote from Ekelund et al. tells the story of the Church position on usury (interest).

> We do not contend that the medieval Church invented the doctrine of usury, or the economic doctrine of just price, for its own gain. Rather, we contend that in spite of its original (and perhaps lasting) concern for justice, the Church recognized, and acted on, the rent seeking opportunities of the doctrine at a certain juncture of its history. We contend that the medieval Church established de facto dual credit markets. When the Church was a lender, it shadow-priced its loans *inside* the Church at market rates (or above), thus extracting rents. But when it was a borrower, it enforced the doctrine, thereby extracting rents by reducing its cost of credits on certain loans....Through selective performance the Church could increase the supply of loan funds available to itself indirectly by reducing the supply of loans for (laic) consumption purposes.... The chief monetary goal of the Church was to increase its ability to finance its salvation effort; its main nonmonetary goal was to preserve and extend its doctrinal hegemony--that is, to increase demand and lower demand elasticity for final output [salvation].[1]

The rent-seeking behavior of the Church contributed to institutional restructuring in the West in two ways. First, the medieval Church used its wealth to finance, among other causes, impressive cultural and economic achievements. Second, the medieval Church kept alive the spirit of entrepreneurship. However, the role of the medieval Church in fostering economic development should not be exaggerated. Manchester wrote: "It says much about the middle ages that in the year 1500, after a thousand years of neglect, the roads built by the Romans were still the best on the continent."[2]

---

[1] R. Ekelund et al., *Sacred Trust*, pp. 115-117.
[2] W. Manchester, *A World Lit Only By Fire*, p. 5.

City-States

Two kinds of cities emerged in the Middle Ages. Some, like Venice, Florence, Genoa and Ragusa, were primarily trading cities and grew into powerful city-states. To survive competition from other cities, major trading centers had to provide credible guarantees of enforcement of property rights as well as a law of commercial contracts.

Other cities developed around medieval castles. A castle was the home of a local lord and the fortress where people sought shelter during an attack. The lord was a semi-autonomous ruler of his feud. And the city was the place peasants went to trade, repair their tools, attend church services, and get together to play, drink and gossip. The major activity of all feuds was agriculture. Since labor was a scarce resource up until the mid-fifteenth century, when the growth of mineral-based industry began to change the economic landscape of Europe, local lords were in competition with one another for the supply of peasants. An important consequence of that competition was that the rights of serfs were secure.

The most important contribution of city-states in the Middle Ages was the enforcement of property rights and laws of contracts across all social classes. No earlier civilization had done that.

Philosophical Factors

The fifteenth century witnessed the revival of interest in the cultural heritage of Rome and Greece. The heritage of Rome was a legal system, which emphasized private property rights and the law of commerce. The heritage of Greece was inquisitive reasoning, which is a springboard for the development of science. Predictably, the revival of interest in the cultural tradition of Rome and Greece triggered the emergence of powerful new ideas, which had to be subversive of all that medieval society had stood for. As William Manchester observes:

> The mighty storm was swiftly approaching, but Europeans were not aware of it....Shackled in ignorance, disciplined by fear, and sheathed in superstition, they trudged into the

sixteenth century...their vacant faces, pocked by smallpox, turned blindly toward the future they thought they knew.[1]

The process of alienation of philosophy from theology started with nominalism in the fourteenth century. Nominalists such as the English philosopher William Occam declared that the gulf between reason and theology might be unbridgeable. The idea of the separation of philosophy from theology gained momentum with the development of the scientific method of looking at the world. Francis Bacon (1561-1626), John Locke (1632-1704) and David Hume (1711-1776), among others, raised the issue of the supremacy of reason and knowledge over the revealed truth. Their method of analysis was experimentation and the objective was to enhance knowledge. Bacon argued for the progress of science and its application to human life. Locke thought that the state should support natural laws and that within this structure the individual should have free rein. Hume argued for private property rights.

On the continent, Rene Descartes (1596-1650), Isaac Newton (1642-1727) and August Comte (1798-1857), again among others, emphasized the importance of mathematics and science. Descartes claimed that mathematics could be extended to philosophy. Newton was concerned with the rules of reasoning in philosophy. Comte argued that actual knowledge depends on testing. Immanuel Kant (1724-1804), a leading rationalist in the eighteenth century, insisted on the authority of science.

Philosophical developments in Europe were propelled by the rising desire to improve understanding of the world by emphasizing inquisitive reasoning, science and experimentation. The alienation of philosophy from theology was applied to economic life by Adam Smith, whose famous book *The Wealth of Nations* (1776) marked the beginning of economics as a social science.

The Religious Reformation

In *Protestant Ethics and the Spirit of Capitalism*, Max Weber offered an extensive analysis of the role of reformation on the spiritual and

---

[1] W. Manchester, *A World Lit Only By Fire*, p. 27.

material life of medieval man. The purpose of Weber's analysis was to establish that Luther and especially Calvin played major roles in the rise of capitalism. Weber argued that the Puritan spirit that emerging from Calvin's teaching gave tremendous impetus to the development of the frugal, hardworking and accumulating individual. Weber's analysis is open to serious analytical as well as empirical criticism.

The Weber thesis aside, Martin Luther (1483-1546) and John Calvin (1509-1564) bore the costs of opening up the market for salvation by offering a new interpretation of guidance to the attainment of redemption. Their respective interpretations of the product offered by Christianity passed the market test. But along with losing its monopoly in the market for guidance to the attainment of salvation, the Church monopoly in the temporal world was weakened as well.

New Frontiers

According to Deepak Lal:

> ...voyages of discovery were impelled in part by the need to find an alternative to the ancient trade routes to the East, to obtain the spices which were essential for preserving meat during the long and lean European winters. The traditional routes across the Red Sea, and the Silk Route had been blocked by the territorial expansion of the new Islamic civilization. The voyages of discovery led not only to the extension of the European land frontier through the acquisition of the nearly empty lands--or those which Western arms and disease emptied--in the New World, but also in time to the colonization of most of Africa and Asia by the West.[1]

However, the discovery of new frontiers had an unintended consequence. New philosophy gave birth to new ideas. Yet, tradition in Europe was strong. The old order, with its customs, class privileges, and medieval values, was powerful and resistant to new ideas. The Catholic Church was too deeply rooted in people's minds to be quickly weakened. And Europe was poor and overcrowded; new concepts

---

[1] D. Lal,. *Factor Endowments, Culture and Politics: On Economic Performance in the Long Run*, the Ohlin Memorial Lectures delivered at the Stockholm School of Economics, October 1995, chapter 5, p. 3.

lacked the space to be tried out. The exploration and settlement of new frontiers, primarily in North America, provided an excellent laboratory for new ideas.

The most important contribution of new frontiers to the great transformation of medieval society into the world we know was in providing a tradition-free space in which to test new ideas. Freedom from religious constraints, from humble origins, and from traditional ethics allowed thousands of people to pursue their individual preferences, to take responsibility for their own actions, and to create their own way of life. Once those ideas were applied to everyday life and proven successful, they traveled back to Europe and contributed substantially there to the transformation of the medieval world into modern society.

The people who went to North America in the early days of the new frontiers were often referred to as criminal elements. Indeed, they were criminals by the then prevailing standards, when it was a crime to oppose the established order, reject medieval tradition, complain about the church, and avoid taxes imposed by kings, feudal lords and bishops. Most settlers came to America to escape those restrictions. They had a "rebellious" desire to make their own choices, choose their own morals, and develop their own rules of the game.

Besides providing a tradition-free space for the application of new ideas, the new frontiers made an additional contribution to the great transformation. Of every $100 worth of gold and silver produced in Western Europe and the New World after 1492, $85 worth was produced in the new frontiers. Taking precious metals and other goods to Europe was quite risky but also quite profitable-- enough to ensure that it happened. An unintended result of this individual risk-taking was to give new ideas a chance to demonstrate their social and economic consequences.

Sociological Factors

The great transformation required a middle class, a supply of labor, and a positive attitude toward work--none of which existed, in an institutional sense, in the Middle Ages.

The medieval nobility could not supply entrepreneurship. Its concerns were wars, politics, and leisure. It was degrading for a nobleman to engage in commercial activities, trade and crafts. He was born to be a lord, a hunter, a lover, and a warrior. Entrepreneurship emerged from the ranks of small traders and artisans. Those people were envious of all the status, privileges, and wealth enjoyed by the nobility. They also wanted to draw a line between themselves and the lower class of peasants. In the quest for status and influence, small traders and artisans turned their energies toward the accumulation of wealth. Eventually, they laid out the foundation for the emergence of an entrepreneurial class.

The labor force emerged from several sources. The rate of population growth in Europe in the aftermath of the Black Death (during the fourteenth century) was an important factor. With an increase in the population, the marginal productivity of serfs fell relative to the value of land. This change in the economic conditions of life provided incentives for the land-owning aristocracy to seek to replace the feudal system of nontransferable ownership that tied peasants to their land with private, transferable ownership of land. Enclosures and other methods of throwing peasants off the land were an important source of labor. Among other factors that led to an increase in the supply of labor were improvements in health care, the gradual disappearance of private armies and guilds, and the advent of child labor.

In the scheme of social values that prevailed in the Middle Ages, begging and physical labor were considered two acceptable methods of survival for the poor. The religious reformation was largely responsible for developing a positive attitude toward work. By giving strong religious sanctions to hard work, the Reformation divorced productive work from welfare. A person's attitude toward work became a measure of character and integrity.

Capital Formation

On the supply side, two major sources of investable funds are private savings and bank credit. Neither existed in the Middle Ages. Private wealth was spent on the church, palaces, private armies, luxuries, purchasing insurance policies (e.g., building cathedrals), and many other activities, or was reserved for heirs.

The Reformation had strong influence on the supply of private savings. To prove themselves chosen for salvation and to avoid temptations, people had to work hard and live frugally. This religious sanction for the accumulation of wealth opened the door for private savings.

Medieval banks did not give credit. Their major function was to safeguard deposits and transfer them from one account to another. According to Joseph Schumpeter, the failure of medieval banks to create bank credit was a major reason that Italian cities such as Florence, Genoa and Venice were not able to sustain their prosperity. The development of the modern banking system began in 1694, when the Bank of England was founded. It gained momentum in 1797, when the British government forbade the bank to pay its notes in gold, opening the door to a rapid increase in the volume of bank credit. When the gold standard was reimposed in 1821, the ability of banks to create credit, a vital source of capital formation, was firmly established.

BASIC FEATURES OF CAPITALISM

The system that slowly emerged from the old one, beginning in the fifteenth century, was a consequence of many factors including advance of scientific method, competitive entries into the market for salvation, new discoveries, rise of entrepreneurship, developments of capital market, and bank credit. Adam Smith described the new system, which he called the Natural System of Economic Liberty, as being self-generating, self-propelling, and self-regulating. Some people called it laissez-faire. Property rights scholars refer to it as the private property, free-market economy. Marxists and pro-Marxists, with a tone of ethical and social disapproval, named the system capitalism. And the name they coined has prevailed.

The two cornerstones of capitalism are classical liberalism and methodological individualism. Classical liberalism is about individual liberty, openness to new ideas, tolerance of all views, private property rights, the rule of law, and the freedom of contracts. Methodological individualism says that only individuals make decisions. To understand decisions within governments, corporations and other types of organizations, it is necessary to recognize decision makers in those organizations, pay attention to their private ends, and identify the incentives under which they work. Neither organizations nor committees make decisions. There is always an individual who conceives an idea, formulates it into a rule or policy, and convinces other members of the organization or committee to accept it.

Individual liberty, openness to new ideas, and tolerance of the values held by others create an environment in which individuals are free to pursue their private ends. The rule of law provides equal protection for all individuals to pursue those ends. Private property rights and the freedom of exchange creates incentives for competing individuals to pursue self-interest, self-determination, self-responsibility and free-market competition. Simply said, capitalism is about letting each individual pursue his or her end, given other individuals' rights to do the same.

The development of capitalism in Europe differed from one country to another and from one region to another (e.g., northern and southern Italy) depending, among other things, on the response of informal institutions to the new system.

EARLY CRITICS OF CAPITALISM

Early Catholic theologians and philosophers raised the issue of the legitimacy of capitalism as a moral system. The origin of these philosophers' unease with the system lies in the basic difference between the Catholic and the capitalist concepts of community. That which a classical liberal considers as the freeing of individuals from the constraints of (medieval) tradition, a conservative Catholic philosopher sees as erosion of morality and rejection of "absolute" values. Conservative Catholic philosophy is apprehensive about freedom of choice not because of any lack of interest in individual liberty but because of a fear that autonomy of individual choices in the free market does not necessarily generate morally satisfying sets of preferences. It ignores the fact that the free market does not generate preferences. Those who are critical of the freedom of individual choice should direct their criticism toward the institutions--such as schools, churches, the streets, households, the media--that participate in the formation of our preferences, rather than toward the free market in which those preferences are merely revealed. Suppressing freedom of choice does not change a person's character. It merely deprives people of an opportunity to choose and bear the cost of their choice (e.g., losing friends). While the free market does not make people moral, it raises the cost of unethical behavior. In the 1920s, Ludwig von Mises addressed the issue of the relationship between the church and capitalism as follows:

> It would be foolish to maintain that Enlightenment, by undermining the religious feelings of the masses, had cleared the way for socialism. On the contrary, it is the resistance which the Church offered to the spread of liberal ideas which has prepared the soil for ...modern socialist thought....Christian socialism has done hardly less than atheist socialism to bring about the present state of confusion.[1]

Judging by three encyclicals issued by pope John Paul II, the Catholic Church still has misgivings about capitalism. In *Laborem Exercens* (1981), the pope identified social justice with the development of labor unions. In *Sollicitude Rei Socialis* (1988), he criticized both classical liberalism and Marxism as being unjust movements. In *Centesimus Annus* (1991), the pope defended the collectivist approach in achieving human rights. Ekelund et al. wrote:

> Official Catholic social and economic policy emphasizes serious restraints on private ownership of property and unlimited acquisition of material goods. It has defended state subsidies to farmers....The ideal society that still shapes Catholic doctrine is that of the feudal state, with its simple technology, its small communal living, and its dedication to things spiritual.... Fundamental Church doctrine is antithetical to Smith's concept of self-interest as the guiding motive of capitalism.[2]

Early Socialists

Sir Thomas More (1478-1535) was the first significant critic of capitalism. In his writing, More tried to tie socialist ideas to the moral teachings of the early Church fathers.

More opposed the transformation of the traditional society into a money economy. He realized that the world was changing but argued

---

[1] L. Mises, *Socialism* (Indianapolis: Liberty Fund, Inc.), pp. 379-81.
[2] R. Ekelund et al. *Sacred Trust*, p. 184.

that changes must be made within the bounds of the moral teachings of the church. On a practical level, he believed in primitive communism. Medieval philosophers and early socialists defined primitive communism as a society in which all resources are held in common and no member of the community is allowed to accumulate private wealth. By establishing common ownership of all resources, More believed, the problems of the emerging industrial society could be resolved or avoided. More also believed that private property rights make a just government impossible. Private property rights, he claimed, lead to social inequalities, which generate behaviors that are contrary to divine law.

More's alternative to the emerging capitalist society was the concept of *utopia*. In utopia, agriculture was the most important industry. All citizens, including those living in the cities, must spend some time working on collective farms. The supply of goods for all cities was to be calculated in advance, and their citizens would have to work on the farms in proportion to their cities' food needs. Every month a member of each family would be required to take goods produced by the family to the market. In exchange, the family would receive coupons which it would exchange for other goods in the market. To travel from one community to another would require permission. And the traveler would have to do a day's work at the destination.

In the seventeenth and eighteenth centuries, France became fertile ground for socialist ideas. Unlike Thomas More, who wanted to retreat from capitalism and return to the customs and morality of the old order, French socialists accepted the reality of the rising industrial society and raised a question: What can be done to eliminate the social and economic inequalities of capitalism?

Comte Henri de Saint Simon (1760-1825) and Pierre Joseph Proudhon (1809-1865) were the most prominent among French socialists. Saint Simon participated in the American Revolution and was decorated for bravery during the battle of Yorktown. His primary objective was to find a way to guarantee equal opportunity rather than economic equality. And Saint Simon believed that the only way to achieve equal opportunity was through collective ownership. As a result of his conclusion, he directed his major criticism of capitalism at private property rights. Long before Marx, Saint Simon advocated "from each according to his ability; to each according to his contribution." Like all other socialists, Proudhon opposed private property rights. But, unlike Saint Simon, he believed in actual economic equality.

Robert Owen (1771-1858) is usually called the father of British socialism. Like most early socialists, Owen blamed private property rights for unemployment, child labor, poverty, and poor working conditions. He believed that the primary objective of human existence is to be happy but, he claimed, happiness cannot be obtained individually. In fact, he argued that competition and individualism lead to the degradation of labor. The remedy he proposed was communism, which would prohibit private property rights.

What was the common denominator in the ideas of early socialist thinkers? They all believed that a happy and harmonious community was possible. However, they saw private property rights as destroying this natural harmony and, as a consequence, preventing the happiness of the individual. They saw *human reason* as a vehicle for rediscovering the world of peace and harmony. Harry Laidler, a student of socialism, wrote in 1927:

> Social change was regarded by [early socialists] as largely a result of the social discovery of brilliant men. If some one in society five hundred years before their time had discovered the truths which they were proclaiming, and had explained these truths to their fellowmen, misery and suffering, they felt, would long since have disappeared. For absolute truth is independent of time, space...and it is thus a mere accident when and where it is discovered. [Early socialists] also had the mistaken notion that it was possible for social thinkers to cut out a pattern of a future order in all of its details, and that mankind could be induced to follow faithfully every detail of that pattern.[1]

THE RISE OF SOCIALISM

Socialism, as the world experienced that system in the twentieth century, cannot be divorced from the teachings of Karl Marx. Perhaps the application of socialism was at variance with Marx's hopes and aspirations. Jesus would probably have the same problem with the

---

[1] H. Laidler, *A History of Socialist Thought* (New York: Thomas Crowell Co. 1927), p. 139.

application by Christian churches of his teachings. However, the founders of movements and ideologies cannot avoid being responsible for the consequences of their teachings.

Karl Marx (1818-1883) was born in the Rhineland of Germany. He was one of seven children in a Jewish family that embraced Christianity when he was six years of age. Marx studied philosophy, history, law and literature in Bonn and Berlin. Eventually, he became the most influential critic of capitalism. He was a prolific writer whose contributions cannot be easily summarized in a few pages. This section briefly reviews the sources of influence on Marx and his analysis of the process of social change.

The Sources of Influence on Marx.

Marx was influenced by three contemporary movements: early (French) socialism, classical German philosophy, and classical British economics.

French socialists believed that capitalism was an immoral system. They blamed it for long working hours, child labor, the poverty of working people, unemployment, income inequalities, social injustice, and other problems. And they placed the ultimate blame for these problems on private property rights. Thus, French socialists argued that the simplest way to do away with capitalism and the ills to which it seemed tied to was to abolish private property rights.

Marx agreed with French socialists that capitalism was not a just system. He also agreed with their criticism of private property rights. However, Marx considered it naive to think that socialism, once discovered by reason, could conquer the world simply by promising justice and harmony. He drew a line between the preference for socialism and the scientific analysis of its role in human history. Marx's analysis of the concept of alienated labor, one of his key concepts, explains this point:

Since it does not belong to him or her, the product of a worker's labor appears to that worker to be an alien object; Consequently, the worker considers his work to be imposed labor, and is thus alienated from the work activity; What distinguishes people from animals is our consciousness and self-awareness as regards our life activity, including work--but alienated labor turns a key life activity into a mere means of subsistence, thus alienating people from their species life; The worker is alienated from the owner of the means of production, who owns the product of that worker's labor; Workers and owners, alienated from each other, belong to identifiable social classes. The class struggle is thus a major consequence of private property rights.

The great thinkers of the Middle Ages considered the universe as constant and eternal. Eventually, scholars began to realize that human history is an endless evolution of social institutions. This discovery that the universe is not immutable generated interest in the process of social change. G.W. Friedrich Hegel (1770-1831) was a leading philosopher among those who tried to formulate a theory of social change. His central thesis was that prevailing ideas determine our perceptions about the world in which we live. These common ideas shape our social institutions, the way we interact with each other, and the organization of production and distribution of goods. The essence of Hegel's philosophical method was the concept of dialectics: Each idea has its internal contradiction, and within each idea there is a conflict between its positive and negative elements. It is from this internal conflict inherent in all ideas that a new idea eventually emerges. This new idea is not an extension of the old one. Being a qualitatively different concept, the new idea slowly but surely reshapes all aspects of social life.

Marx accepted Hegel's thesis that human history is shaped by social changes generated from within the social system itself. However, he disagreed with Hegel as to the role of ideas in producing social changes. Marx asserted that the economic conditions of life determine our social institutions, politics, philosophy, religion and ideas. That is, Marx moved Hegel's concept of progress from the sphere of ideas to the material world. Quite appropriately, Marx's method of analysis is called *dialectical materialism*. It says that the process of social change, which occurs through a struggle of positive and negative elements within the prevailing system, consists of the gradual accumulation of small quantitative changes that lead to a major qualitative change in the system. For example, private property rights are the positive element in capitalism, while the proletariat is its negative element (i.e., internal contradiction). In the "dialectical" struggle between private property rights and the rising proletariat, the latter has to triumph. Socialism, a qualitatively different system, will then replace capitalism by abolishing both the proletariat and private property rights.

Marx was also influenced by David Ricardo (1770-1823), from whom he borrowed the labor theory of value. This theory basically said that the value of any commodity is proportional to the average number of labor hours needed for its production. Thus, only labor creates new value; the contribution of capital to the value of a product is equal to its wear and tear. For example, under the labor theory of value, a serving of beer would be worth twice as much as a soft drink if its production required twice as many labor hours.

Marx modified the labor theory of value to suit his purpose. He said that if the value of any good is determined by the average number of hours needed for its production, the value of labor must also be determined by the average number of hours needed for its production. Each day workers use up a certain amount of their energy, which must be replenished so that they are able to work the next day. They must also be able to support their children, who will eventually replace them in the labor force. The market wage, then, is the amount of money that is just sufficient to buy the minimum bundle of goods needed for a worker's maintenance. The value of this bundle of goods is the average number of labor hours needed to produce it.

Suppose the working day is ten hours, but that it takes only five hours to produce the minimum bundle of goods a worker must receive each day. In ten hours, that worker creates the value that brings the employer (i.e., the property owner) an amount of money equal to ten labor-hours. The employer pays the worker a wage that is equal to the value of five labor-hours. The difference between the number of hours the worker labors each day and the number of hours it takes to produce the minimum bundle of goods that worker must have each day is the *surplus value*. The surplus value is captured by the class of property owners.

The Process of Social Change

Marx believed that economic processes explain all of human history, which he saw as a continuous struggle against nature. Triggered by our survival instinct (we would say today by our desire for utility), the struggle has as its ultimate purpose the reversal of the original relationship between human beings and nature.

The sequence begins with primitive society. There, people were totally dependent for their economic survival on an alien and hostile environment. All efforts in a primitive society were geared toward the restricted objective of subsistence; that is, toward the appropriation of products in their natural state. Without innovation, primitive society would merely have reproduced itself through time. However, the survival instinct led people to seek ways to produce subsistence more efficiently. The discovery of fire increased the importance of fish as a source of nourishment, development of the bow and arrow increased returns from hunting, etc. As people learned how to use intermediate goods (tools) to increase the supply of food for subsistence, two related developments had to occur.

First, each time a person creates a new tool (primitive hammer or modern computer), humanity takes a step toward freedom from dependence on nature. Human history, then, is a long journey from our complete economic subordination to nature to our ultimate mastery over nature, in his view. This last stage in our journey through history Marx called communism. Marx's communism could be called a world without scarcity. At any rate, the economic interpretation of history has a strong pseudo-religious content: salvation will happen in this space and time.

Second, as people learned to produce and use tools, it became necessary for them to regulate access to those tools. To define who has what access to an asset means to define property rights in that asset. Thus, Marx deduced the development of property rights from the initial human alienation from nature, and our (survival) instinct to reverse that relationship. Property rights did not develop because a few "wise" souls discovered their importance.

Marx used two general concepts to explain the process of social change leading to the final stage of communism: (1) The productive forces represent the relation between people and nature in the production of goods and services. Marx included in this concept technology, the supply of resources, the work ethic, education, and the relations of production or property relations. (2) The relations of production or property relations are the relations among people in the process of production. Today, we would probably call these a social system. Throughout human history, the relations of production are relations among aliens.

How does the process of social change work? In its journey through history, humanity must pass through definite types of property relations. Given the prevailing property relations (i.e., the social system), our survival instinct brings about incremental improvements in the productive forces. The (historical) purpose of those improvements is to continue to reduce our dependence on nature. However, at some level of economic development, the prevailing property relations will become a fetter to further improvements in the productive forces. Then and only then, the prevailing social system has performed its historical function. As the old system breaks down, a qualitatively new set of property rights will emerge. This new system will accelerate improvements in the forces of production (i.e., economic development). But, at some level of economic development, the system that was initially a progressive one will once again become an obstacle to further improvements in the forces of production. The cycle repeats itself until the final stage of communism is reached. According to Marx, in its journey through history, mankind must pass through definite types of property relations (i.e., socio-economic systems). A system cannot be born before the old one has performed its historical function.

It is probably safe to assert that few people today subscribe to Marx's thesis of the inevitability of socialism. Empirical experiences with all kinds of socialist institutions--ranging from those of the former USSR to those in Cuba, the former Yugoslavia, Allende's Chile, and China--have not been very helpful in upholding faith in the inevitability of socialism. The bankruptcy of socialism in the former Soviet Union and Eastern European supports neither Marx's analysis of the process of social change nor his thesis that socialism is inevitable. To salvage Marxism, socialists have to rewrite Marx's doctrine or replace the founding father.

SOCIALISM

The rejection of private property rights was the central premise of socialism from its earliest days. Marx and other founding fathers of socialism attributed unemployment, income inequalities, child labor, poverty, and most other social and economic problems of early capitalism to the effects of the right of ownership. Predictably, abolition of private property rights was the driving ideological force behind all socialist experiments in the twentieth century.

The attitude of present-day socialists has been affected by two real world experiences: the failure of all socialist experiments to develop an efficient set of institutions, and the theoretical research and empirical evidence about the efficiency-enhancing consequences of the right of ownership. Those two factors have created strong (survival) incentives for socialists to rewrite the doctrine in a way that would make private property rights and socialism compatible. This means that contemporary socialists must go back to drawing boards and try to develop a new set of socialist institutions.

In the meantime, positive analysis of socialism must address the consequences of two sets of institutional arrangements that were in place long enough to be identified with socialism: the system of central planning and the labor-managed economy. The best examples of those institutional arrangements are the former Soviet Union and the former Yugoslavia. Apologists for socialism argue that by pursuing their own ends, the political leadership in the USSR and Yugoslavia ruined the chance for socialism to prove itself as a viable alternative to the free-market, private property economy. That is a correct argument. In order to explain the behavior of the ruling elite, economic analysis should assume that the leaders of the Soviet Union and Yugoslavia pursued their own private ends *within* the system of incentives embedded in socialist institutions.

The system of central economic planning and the labor-managed economy were not ad hoc models invented by and limited to a few countries. They were the consequence of the basic philosophical and economic premises of the socialist doctrine as it has evolved since the eighteenth century.

THE ROLE OF LAW IN CAPITALISM AND SOCIALISM

Socialism relies on the ability of the political-scientific elite to identify the public interest and to develop the rules that are expected to attain it. Capitalism maintains that individuals are the best judges of their own ends. Where capitalism opposes the coercion of citizens so that they can instead pursue their private ends, socialism seeks to coerce individuals so that the community can attain the intended outcome. To paraphrase Hayek, socialism makes individuals a bare tool in the achievement of the ends of the political-scientific elite. A consequence is that politicians and bureaucrats in a socialist state have significant discretionary power. Such power creates a political market in which individuals have to invest their time and resources either in seeking favorable laws or in averting unfavorable ones.

Socialism sees the free-market, private property economy as encouraging selfishness and greed. Thus, legal rules are needed to avert antisocial behaviors. Capitalism, on the other hand, contends that it is not a function of law to modify individual choices and preferences. Any individual should be free to purchase an antisocial behavior at a market price, which is the cost imposed on the individual by friends and neighbors.

The concepts of fairness, justice and morality have different connotations in capitalism and socialism. A capitalist society puts a premium on the rules that reward performance, cultivate risk-taking attitudes, promote the development of individual liberties, and place value on the keeping of promises. In a socialist society, the terms fairness, justice and morality are used to justify laws that change the distribution of income, provide social insurance coverage, mandate educational choices, and impose price controls. Says George Stigler:

> I deny the existence of a widely accepted, coherent moral code in which non-coercion is an irresistible corollary. The assertion of moral values, in the absence of such a code, is either a disguised expression of personal preferences or a refusal to continue the analysis of a problem.[1]

Capitalism is a *process* within which individuals voluntarily interact in the pursuit of their own private ends and, in doing so, create an order. The spontaneous order that the market achieves is a way of life deriving its energies and behavioral incentives from the right of ownership, contractual freedom, and a government under law. An important positive aspect of this spontaneous order is that the value of resources in their alternative uses is identified by the only source of value: *the individual*. James Buchanan wrote:

> Economic performance can only be conceived in values; but how are values determined? By prices, and prices emerge only in markets. They have no meaning in a non-market context,... where the choice-influenced opportunity costs are ignored.[2]

---

[1] J. Stigler, "Wealth, and Possibly Liberty," *Journal of Legal Studies* 9 (1980), p. 216.

[2] J. Buchanan, "General Implications of Subjectivism in Economics," Paper presented at the Conference on Subjectivism in Economics, Dallas, Texas, December 1976.

It is misleading to consider capitalism and socialism as alternative mechanisms for the allocation of resources. They represent two different ways of life, each having specific and predictable effects on the development of laws and regulations. In evaluating the institutions of socialism, critical questions are: Can socialism establish the desirability of outcome-oriented laws? Are those outcomes attainable? At what costs? With respect to capitalism, important questions are: What are the incentives for the spontaneous development of laws? What are the expected consequences of those rules? And at what costs?

SUGGESTED READING
R. Ekelund, R. Hebert, R. Tollison, G. Anderson, and A Davidson, *Sacred Trust: The Medieval Church as an Economic Firm* (Oxford: Oxford University Press, 1996).

D. North, and R. Thomas, *The Rise of the Western World* (Cambridge: Cambridge University Press, 1973).

PART THREE

PROPERTY RIGHTS, EXCHANGE AND PRODUCTION

Chapter 7

PRIVATE PROPERTY RIGHTS, EXCHANGE AND PRODUCTION

In chapters three to six, we discussed the competitive process that is carried out by means of the development and choice of rules individuals adopt as the instruments with which they compete. The competitive process within the prevailing rules is a knowledge-creating process. It continuously creates and spreads knowledge about opportunities for human interaction. This chapter discusses the implications of the right of ownership on exchange and production.

EXCHANGE

Exchange is a means by which individuals seek more satisfaction for themselves. The method of payment by one of the parties could be money or other goods; in exchange for using my lawn mower, a neighbor might drive my kids to school. People enter into exchange because they *expect* that their *benefits* from acquiring a good will exceed their *costs*. To understand the purpose of exchange it is important to understand the three terms emphasized here.

    The benefit from exchange is the increment in satisfaction a person derives from acquiring the right to use a little more of any good. The value of any good to a person depends on the expected flow of benefits and the bundle of rights being transferred. New knowledge about exchange opportunities affects the price by modifying our perception of the expected flow of benefits from that good. Once a person discovers that he loves Czech beer, schlitz would have to lower the price to keep that person business. And changes in the bundle of rights in a good that is being exchanged affect the price we are willing to pay for that good. The value of a car to me is less if I have no right to resell it; I pay more to join a country club if my teenage kids are allowed to play golf there; and I value my house more if I have a right to exclude gasoline stations from the neighborhood.

The cost of exchange is the satisfaction a person has to give up. When someone spends $50 on shoes, the real cost of the shoes is the satisfaction that would be available from another bundle of goods that $50 could buy. By going out on a date the evening before an exam, a student gives up the satisfaction of a higher grade that several hours of additional study could have made possible. In general, the cost of exchange is the value of that which is being given up (i.e., opportunity cost).

In a world of uncertainty and incomplete information, the future consequences of our current decisions can only be anticipated. A pair of shoes might fall apart within a few days, a BMW might turn out to be a lemon, and things might not get better with Coke. Individuals form their own subjective perceptions about future consequences of specific exchange opportunities. Those perceptions are likely to differ from one person to another. Thus, some would choose to negotiate exchanges that other find unattractive.

The Terms and Extent of Exchange

To say that exchange makes us better off does not mean that people carry with them small computers to calculate the increments of satisfaction they expect to derive from each and every exchange. Sometimes we agonize over a decision (e.g., choosing a major), sometimes we act on impulse (e.g., hitting a friend), and sometimes we act out of habit (i.e., buying the same brand of cigars). However, human behavior is consistent in one respect. The bundle of other things that a person is willing to give up in exchange for one unit of a good depends upon preference and income. Given the satisfaction I expect to get from Czech beer, a reduction in its price would induce me to drink more beer because the bundle of other things I have to give up is now less. That might change when I discovers Coors beer.

The importance of income is, however, easy to exaggerate. For example, even though you have $1,000 to spend, you may choose to forgo a second cup of coffee if its price increases from fifty cents to a dollar. The satisfaction you derive from other goods (e.g., beer) that one dollar can buy is the major factor affecting the exchange you choose. Income is primarily a constraint that defines your set of choices.

Suppose an important high-school football game is played in your town. The game is a sellout. Bill was somehow able to get a ticket at the regular price of $20. He is quite happy, because he would have been willing to pay as much as $30 for the ticket; a situation that might change if he were to discover that the new coach of his home team is a poor teacher. But, given his incomplete information, Bill prefers $31 worth of other goods to watching the game. He has four neighbors who are in the same income bracket but differ in the satisfaction they expect to derive from watching the game. Table 7-1 shows the maximum price they are willing pay for tickets.

Table 7-1. The Demand for Tickets

Neighbor 1	$70
Neighbor 2	$60
Neighbor 3	$50
Neighbor 4	$40
Bill	$30

Here we have five people who value the same good differently. *They do not know each other's preferences for watching the game. Knowledge of other people's utility functions is not available to a decision maker*. And standard assumptions such as given relative prices and/or given utility functions are misleading. Those variables do not exist independently from the action-choosing process through which they are generated. As they seek more utility for themselves, individuals reveal their preferences and modify them as they acquire new knowledge about exchange opportunities.

Not knowing Bill's preference for watching the game, neighbor 4 offers $28 for the ticket. Bill turns the offer down because he prefers watching the game to whatever else $28 could buy. However, neighbor 4 has incentives to raise his offer. If and when he offers more than $30, he gets the ticket. Depending on Bill's and neighbor 4's respective bargaining skills (and luck), the price will end up somewhere between $30 and $40. Neighbors 3 and 2 have incentives to raise the offer to $41 and $51 respectively. By raising the offer above $60, say to $64, neighbor 1 will eventually get the ticket. Bill is better off because in exchange for something that to him is worth $30, he gets a bundle of goods worth $64. Neighbor 1 is better off because he gives up a bundle of goods worth $64 in exchange for watching the game that he values at $70. And no one in the community is worse off.

The allocation of the ticket does not depend on prior knowledge (perfect foresight) of what each person is willing to pay for the opportunity to watch the game. The price emerges through the choice-making process in a world of incomplete information. By raising their successive offers, those who value the ticket more bribe those who value it less to withdraw from competition.

Raising the price does not create more tickets but Bill ends up with a large profit. However, the price above $60 is necessary in order to allocate the ticket (a scarce good) to a person who values watching the game most. The ticket might change hands several times on its journey to the highest bidder. For example, the outcome would have been the same if neighbor 4 had been able to purchase the ticket from Bill for, say, $36. Neighbor 2 would then bid the ticket away from him for any price in excess of $50, and so on. Neighbor 1 would still get the ticket, but the gains from trade would be shared by several people.

In either case, the ticket is allocated to the highest bidder. All exchange opportunities are exploited and the extent of exchange is maximized (the allocation of resources is efficient). There is no additional exchange that could make one person better off without making another worse off. Moreover, the value that each of them attaches to watching the game is based on their respective subjective perceptions of the benefits. The competitive process being a knowledge-creating process, those benefits are subject to revisions from one game to another. Their knowledge about each other's preference for watching the game remains incomplete.

The Law of Demand

Clearly an inverse relationship exists between the price of a good and the quantity of that good demanded. This proposition is known as the law of demand. The law of demand captures the essence of human behavior in a world of scarcity: people demand more of any good at a lower price and less of that good at a higher price. The law of demand then is one of the most important concepts in economic analysis.

The explanatory and predictive powers of the law of demand arise from its verifiability. A car dealer gives you a better discount when the lot is full of cars for sale. Fresh fruits costs less in season than out of season. When a retail store wants to move some merchandise faster, the manager advertises a lower price. Students have fewer dates the evening before a major exam than the day after. An increase in the price of crime (i.e., the joint probability of getting caught, being convicted, and kept in jail) reduces the rate of criminal activity. At a higher price for shoes, we wear them longer. At a higher price of gasoline, we make fewer trips and eventually look for a smaller car. Adjustments to changes in the variables that affect costs and benefits of using a good are always costly. The more time we have to make adjustments, the lower is the cost of making adjustments. In price theory, we summarize this by saying that the demand of any good tends to get more elastic in the long run.

Some people claim that there are exceptions from the law of demand. The fact that it takes time to find examples that are not consistent with the law of demand confirms its general validity, however. Economic analysis is more concerned with what we routinely observe than with things that are possible. To paraphrase Armen Alchian, what is the purpose of seeking an exception from the behavior that we constantly observe?

The Demand Schedule

Let us return to our example. The demand schedule for football tickets is summarized in Table 7-2.

Table 7-2. Five-Person Demand for Tickets

Price	Bill	N'bor 1	N'bor 2	N'bor 3	N'bor 4	Total
>70	0	0	0	0	1	1
>60	0	0	0	1	1	2
>50	0	0	1	1	1	3
>40	0	1	1	1	1	4
>30	1	1	1	1	1	5

We can use information in Table 7-2 to draw a standard diagram on the demand schedule for tickets by plotting quantities demanded against prices. The demand schedule shows the quantity of a good that is demanded per unit of time or activity (e.g., football game), all other things such as property rights, preferences, incomes, and prices of other goods being given. The effect of changes in those factors is to shift the demand schedule in one or the other direction. For example, making nontransferable a currently transferable property right to cut a given quantity of trees in a public forest would reduce the price of that right. However, while the law of demand is a general proposition that accurately describes human behavior, the demand schedule for a good attempts to provide specific information on how much of that good is going to be bought at each given price. With positive transaction costs as well as the continuous knowledge-creating process of market competition, all that we really know about the demand schedule for any specific good is that more of that good is bought at lower than at higher prices. Even if we were able to learn what the demand schedule of a good actually is, we would only have learned what it was.

The demand schedule of a good is always drawn sloping down to the right. Because its slopes conform to the law of demand, it has become one of the most useful tools in economic analysis.

Exchange and Nonpecuniary Goods

We observe that some exchange opportunities are not exploited even though their transaction costs are low. It is wrong to interpret those cases as the failure of private property rights to move resources to their higher-valued uses. People derive satisfaction from a number of specific goods, such as a pleasant environment, congenial colleagues, friendly neighbors, and clean air. Those are scarce goods; that is, we purchase them at a price. I might prefer Dallas to New York, humble colleagues in a second-rate academic department to self-centered scholars is a great department, an ethnic neighborhood to a mixed neighborhood, and polluted air in Dallas to fresh country air in College Station.

The satisfaction we derive from nonpecuniary goods has its pecuniary income equivalent. An additional $5,000 per year would not make me move from Dallas to New York. But $50,000 would. Or suppose I own a house with an apartment to rent. A widow with five children offers to pay $500 per month for that apartment, while a plumber offers $450. I might decide that to have a friendly plumber around is worth more to me than $50 per month. But for $600 per month the widow with kids could get the apartment. The satisfaction we receive from purchasing specific goods is subjective and has its money income equivalent.

Charitable giving is also a source of satisfaction. When I give $10 to the boy scouts I am saying that the satisfaction I derive from that exchange is more important to me than whatever satisfaction I could get from another bundle of goods that $10 could buy. The fact that we discriminate in making contributions is evidence that they are made in the pursuit of our self-interest. We give to those people and institutions whose happiness is important to us. Charitable giving also conforms to the law of demand. A tax reduction makes charitable giving more expensive and people give less.

PRODUCTION

Production means using goods to produce other goods. Thus production is exchange. However, production has enough specific properties to warrant a separate hearing. It is customary to refer to the goods required to produce other goods as resources. Like all other goods, resources have alternative uses. The cost of producing one unit of any good, then, is the market value of other goods the same bundle of resources could have produced in the same time period. For example, the costs of making Charlie into a good friend--that is, the costs of producing a friend--are my time (that is, the value of an alternative activity) and the money I spend going out with him (that is, the value of a bundle of other goods the same amount of money could purchase).

Private Property Rights and Production

Suppose that five entrepreneurs are producing video cassette recorders. Table 7-3 shows the quantity of VCRs that each can produce per unit of time, and their opportunity costs in terms of the market value of alternative outputs that have to be given up. The costs of producing VCRs thus include the payments that each producer has to make for the right to use resources that belong to other people (labor, parts, glass, etc.), as well as the value of their own resources in alternative uses.

In a private property economy, no entrepreneur among the five would choose to produce VCRs at any price below $30. They all do better for themselves by producing something else. If and when the price per VCR rises above $30, C would, driven by his desire for more, switch from whatever he was doing to making VCRs. His decision benefits the community as well. At $32 per VCR, C makes a profit of $2 per VCR, while the community gives up $30 worth of other goods in exchange for a VCR which it values at $32.

Table 7-3. Five-Person Production Alternatives

	VCR in units	$ of other Goods	Cost per VCR
A	250	27,500	$110
B	300	27,000	$90
C	100	3,000	$30
D	200	14,000	$70
E	400	20,000	$50

$30 per VCR is the minimum price at which C could produce VCRs, $50 is the minimum price for E, and so on. The result of this interaction between the right of ownership and the desire for more satisfaction produces a supply schedule. *The right of ownership creates incentives for the supply schedule to slope upward to the right.* It shows the minimum price necessary to encourage producers to offer each given quantity of that good for sale. The upward slope of the supply schedule indicates a tendency for the production of VCRs to be efficient. If E were the first to produce VCRs, the community would have wasted $20 worth of other goods per one VCR.

PRIVATE PROPERTY RIGHTS AND PRICE COMPETITION

The demand schedule is not known to those who buy and sell goods. The same goes for the supply schedule. As we have seen, this knowledge is not necessary in a private property economy. The right of ownership provides strong incentives for buyers and producers continuously to seek ways to reduce transaction costs and move their resources to higher-valued uses. The competitive process is thus a knowledge-creating process which continuously and incrementally modifies the subjective perceptions individuals have about their sets of choices and trade-offs.

Data in Table 7-4 are hypothetical and conform to both the law of demand and the incentives effects of private property rights. They illustrate two critical functions of relative prices: to allocate the supply of a good among competing users (who gets what), and to control changes in the supply of that good (who should produce what).

In that sense data in Table 7-4 help us to understand the *tendencies* inherent in the choice-making process in a private property, free-market economy. It is important, however, to bear in mind that the tendencies could only tell us what the equilibrium would have been if those tendencies continued to work during the period of observation and if no other factors (especially new knowledge) intervened. And that is never the case. The properties of the equilibrium-to-be change with changes in knowledge and in other factors that influence our subjective perceptions of reality. And we know that changes in knowledge and those other factors depend on institutional structures and transaction costs. They are not the exogenous constraints of neoclassical theory.

Suppose that the price per VCR is $21 and no VCRs are produced. At that price a number of people prefer VCRs to whatever else $21 could buy. Whether they offer to pay more for VCRs or some producers raise the price in response to observed shortages of VCRs is irrelevant. What is important is that the price is going to be bid up.

As the price is bid to $31 per VCR, two things happen. First, C finds it in his self-interest to produce VCRs. The desire for more satisfaction plus the right to keep the benefits from making VCRs (a component of the right of ownership) provide C with sufficient incentives to respond to the demand for that good at any price above $30. Second, as the price per VCR goes up, some people decide that a VCR is not worth a larger bundle of other things that has to be sacrificed, and switch to other goods. The process of bidding the price higher then reduces the shortage of VCRs.

As the price is bid up to $50, C makes more profit but no additional VCRs reach the market. However, this increase in the price per VCR is necessary for two reasons. First, it helps to induce some people, who like VCRs but not as much as some others do, to drop out of the market (or buy fewer units). Second, an increase in price is necessary to bring in higher-cost producers of VCRs.

At the price of $51, E finds it in her self-interest to begin producing VCRs. She does not know the market demand schedule for VCRs. If she jumps in with both feet and makes only VCRs, the total supply of VCRs (made by C plus E) would increase to 500. At $51 per unit, people are willing to buy only 320 units. E discovers that she cannot sell all that she has produced. She has to stop making VCRs and try to sell her unanticipated inventory of them below the costs of production, or take time to work inventories down, or go bankrupt. As her inventories are depleted, E learns that while she cannot sell 400 VCRs at a profit, she might increase her total earnings by selling *some* units. Suppose that by trial and error, she ends up producing 200 VCRs. The price at which C and E sell the supply of 300 VCRs is $61. C gets rich and E does well, too. Her total revenue is now $22,200 ($12,200 from selling 200 VCRs at $61, and $10,000 from using the rest of her resources to produce other goods), which is better than the $20,000 she made before switching to VCRs.

Table 7-4. Demand and Supply of VCRs

Price in $	Demand for VCRs	Supply of VCRs
141	140	1,250
131	160	1,250
121	180	1,250
111	200	1,250
101	220	1,000
91	240	1,000
81	260	700
71	280	700
61	300	500
51	320	500
41	340	100
31	360	100
21	380	0

Yet, E has incentives to sell additional VCRs at any price above $50 provided that those sales have no effect on the price ($61) at which she sells the first 200 units. Indeed, we observe a number of methods used to reduce transaction costs of negotiating additional exchanges without a reduction in the prevailing market price, such as buying two units of a good at a discount (one suit for $500, two for $650), tie-in sales (50% discount on oil changes for five years when you buy a Honda at Bob's Place), and all sorts of bonuses (a frequent flyer package).

Analogously, the same process of searching for, discovering, and negotiating exchange opportunities takes place when the quantity demanded exceeds the quantity supplied.

OWNERSHIP, INCENTIVES, AND TRANSACTION COSTS

Equilibrium is a situation where all exchange and/or production opportunities have been exploited, where no individuals find it to their advantage to change contractual bargains, and where, consequently, the allocation of resources is efficient. However, the world is full of observations that cast doubts on the usefulness of the concept of equilibrium to enhance our understanding of real world processes. As discussed earlier in this book, by focusing on the maximization paradigm, equilibrium analysis fails to tells us much about the process of adaptation in a world of uncertainty and incomplete knowledge.

Suppose neighbor 1 lives across town. He might never learn about the availability of a ticket at a price he is willing to pay; hence neighbor 2 might end up watching the game. Entrepreneur C might never know that VCRs are being sold at a price above $30 in another marketing area. When I build my house in Texas I might be giving up a higher-valued use for the land (drilling for oil). Positive transaction costs prevent resources from ending up in their more valuable uses.

In a private property economy, people bear the costs and capture the benefits of their decisions. This means that they have incentives to seek new exchange opportunities as well as to modify existing ones, and that they bear the costs of failing to do so. An implication is that exchange opportunities are not given. People have incentives to seek ways to reduce transaction costs, which means that transaction costs are not given either. In short, new opportunities for exchange are continuously created and transaction costs continuously lowered in the choice-making process. Here are a few examples.

1. Scalpers, retail merchants, advertising agencies, real estate companies and, employment bureaus, among others, continuously seek to reduce transaction costs. And they bear the costs of their efforts whenever the gains they capture turn out to be less than their investment in the reduction of transaction costs. An unintended efficiency-enhancing consequence of this process is that resources have a tendency to move from less to more valuable uses.

2. The right of ownership creates incentives for transaction costs to be reduced by those who can do this at a lower cost. Sometimes it is the seller and sometimes it is the buyer. For example, the attributes of many goods are costly to measure. I want to buy oranges to make fresh juice but I do not know which oranges are good for juice and which are better for eating. Or, after a long drive through the state of Montana, I am looking for a comfortable bed in a clean room. Or I want to buy a car but my neighbor tells me about problems he has with his made-in-the United Sates automobile. So am I going to end up choosing less valuable alternatives such as switching to frozen juice, buying a German car, and sleeping in a motel with a nice exterior and dirty rooms? Not necessarily.

Producers of oranges can separate them by quality at a lower cost than I can. And the right of ownership gives them incentives to do that. A motel owner knows that the greater the variability in quality of rooms of average price in the motel industry as a whole, the more valuable is information about the rooms in a particular motel. Out of self-interest, the motel owner might associate with a chain that has a widely known set of standards. When I see a sign for Ramada Inn I know, with a small variance, what to expect. A hotel down the road could be both better and cheaper, but the cost of driving around to purchase additional information about the quality of independent motels could be quite high relative to the certainty of checking into a brand-name establishment.

In the case of many durable goods, the cost of measuring the variability of quality around the average value is reduced as the goods are used. The buyer is then a cheaper provider of information about the attributes of cars, VCRs, television sets, and many other durable goods. By offering customers all kinds of longer warranties, guarantees, and return privileges, the seller reduces transaction costs (i.e., total costs, too) by shifting the quality control to customers. If American-made cars have more problems than German cars but offer more comprehensive and longer warranties, those problems do not necessarily signal a lower quality of American cars but may rather indicate an efficient trade-off between the seller and the buyer that lowers the total cost per car.

3. When I go to a department store to open a credit account, I am invited to sign a contract that offers a pre-determined (standardized) set of terms. How are those terms arrived at? Do they reflect a monopoly (take-it-or-leave-it) power of the store over me?

Clearly, another store could compete for my business by offering better terms. Competition forces all stores to seek and offer contractual terms that satisfy the preferences of the median consumer in their markets. Standardized contracts emerge spontaneously as a method for reducing transaction costs by enabling the parties to avoid the cost of negotiating the terms of contract for each and every exchange they make.

THE ROLE OF PROFIT

The high cost of information, positive transaction costs, and various property rights impede the transfer of resources in the direction of greater efficiency. Yet, every society must tackle the problems of identifying the best uses for resources and transferring resources from lower- to higher-valued uses. Some sort of authority is expected to look after those problems in a socialist state. In capitalism, profit performs this function.

Profits are earnings per period of time in excess of the opportunity costs of resources used in production. Suppose the interest on government bonds is 8 percent. If a business in which you invested $1,000 gives you $60 per year after all direct costs are paid, you lost $20. The cost of investing $1,000 in that business must include the $80 you could have obtained by investing in government bonds. If the business yields $90 after direct costs are paid, your profit is $10. In other words, profit is the amount over and above what a resource could earn in the best alternative use adjusted for risks (that is why the rate of interest on government bonds is usually used as a measure of the best alternative). In a private property economy, those annual profits can be taken out in one lamp sum by selling the assets that generated them. The value of the asset is the expected stream of profits discounted at the market rate of interest.

In a private property economy, changes in profits provide quick, reliable and low-cost information about changes in relative prices and preferences. For example, suppose that people shift their preference between hamburgers and pizza in favor of the latter. The demand for pizza would increase relative to the demand for hamburgers. The resulting change in relative prices of pizza and hamburgers would affect profit rates in those two industries. The rate of return on one dollar's worth of resources in the pizza industry would increase relative to the rate of return in the hamburger industry. The owners of resources have incentives to respond to this information by transferring their assets from lower-valued uses (hamburgers) to higher-valued uses (pizza).

Positive profits in the pizza industry would eventually be whittled away through competition that lowers the price of pizza (larger supplies of pizza) and raises the value of resources used in the production of pizza (larger demand for those resources). However, the competitive process continuously creates, modifies and changes knowledge *specific* to new exchange opportunities. We observe the consequences of those changes in knowledge as innovations, imitation of successful innovations, lower transaction costs of making pizza, new types of pizza, new methods of baking pizza, and new ingredients.

SUMMARY

The government does not have to say: "There shall be price competition." Price competition simply happens whenever the right of ownership and contractual freedom are enforced. The right of ownership and contractual freedom create incentives for individuals (1) spontaneously to negotiate contractual agreements that move resources to their higher-valued uses, (2) spontaneously to seek new opportunities for exchange and production, and (3) spontaneously to seek ways to reduce transaction costs. It is in that sense--the effects of its institutions on economic performance *via* incentives and transaction costs--that capitalism is an efficient system.

SUGGESTED READING

A. Alchian and W. Allen, *Exchange and Production* (Belmont: Wadsworth Publishing Co, 1983), chapters 3-5

C. Ferguson, *The Neoclassical Theory of Production and Distribution* (Cambridge: Cambridge University Press, 1969), chapters 1-6.

Chapter 8

RESTRICTIONS ON OWNERSHIP, EXCHANGE, AND PRODUCTION

Most private property, free-market countries practice one or another form of restriction on private property rights and contractual freedom. This chapter discusses the effects of those that are most frequent: price controls, rationing, market entry restraints, and restrictions on open markets for labor.

PRICE CONTROLS

Suppose that the United States government decides to impose a ceiling on the price of a good. A legal implication of the government's action is that it attenuates (weakens) the right of ownership. The government interferes with the right of all owners (suppliers) to transfer their property rights in that good to other individuals at a mutually agreed upon price. The most frequent justification for price controls is that at a lower price, more people could afford the good. This means that the price of the good is set below its competitive market price. Price controls then create the excess demand for goods that are subject to price controls. What are the economic implications of price controls?

If the maximum price per football ticket in the case discussed earlier is set at $45, the quantity demanded at that price would be three tickets and the quantity supplied would be one. By selling his ticket at $45, Bill is better off. He exchanges watching the game that is worth $30 to him for a bundle of goods that is worth $45. However, Bill is not as well off as he would have been if he were free to exchange his ticket at a freely negotiated price (remember it was $64).

Bill's monetary (pecuniary) gain at $45 is the same regardless of who buys the ticket. He has no incentives to invest in reducing the transaction costs of discovering the highest-valued user of the ticket, in our case neighbor 1. If he sold the ticket to neighbor 1, Bill would gain less and neighbor 1 would gain more than in our free exchange example. A consequence of price controls is the redistribution of income from those who own goods to those who demand them.

Should Bill choose to trade with neighbors 2 and 3, each of them would be better off because they value the ticket in excess of $35. However, each of them could gain more by selling the ticket to neighbor 1, which is something price controls do not allow them to do. The extent of exchange is reduced, leaving some beneficial exchange opportunities unexploited. Another consequence of price controls is then to eliminate incentives to seek the highest-valued uses for goods.

While price controls eliminate the efficiency effects of price competition as a method for resolving the allocation of goods among competing individuals, they cannot eliminate the fact of scarcity. Bill cannot distribute more tickets than he has--his name is not Jesus. At the price of $45 per ticket, the demand for tickets (3) exceeds the supply (1). Bill, however, has to decide who is to get the ticket. What are his choice for resolving the issue of who gets the ticket?

Bill has a choice among several different methods of competition that we observe in most economies today. He could give it on a *first-come, first-served basis,* a frequently observed method for allocating some goods. This type of competition discriminates against people who cannot withstand long hours in a queue or who cannot afford time to do that. For example, a student, an unemployed worker, a housewife, a retired person or a university professor could find it less expensive in terms of other activities to wait in line for the ticket than would a medical doctor, the CEO of a corporation, a plumber, a successful lawyer, and other professionals, who might have to forgo several hundreds of dollars by taking time away from work to wait in line for the ticket.

A medical doctor, driven by self-interest, might hire a retired person to wait in the line as long as the total of the controlled price of the ticket plus payment to the person waiting in line is less than the value of the game to the doctor. The first-come, first-served method of competition then creates incentives to develop two types of markets: a black market for goods that are subject to price controls, and a market for hiring people to wait in line for goods that are in short supply.

Bill could also ask his three neighbors to fight it out among themselves (fists only) with the winner getting the ticket at $45. Throughout human history, *violence* has been a frequently used method for resolving the issue of who gets what. In the first edition of *University Economics*, Armen Alchian and William Allen wrote:

Before rejecting the desirability of violence as a means of competition, a hard-headed student will observe that it has often been a highly respected and widely practiced technique. When Caesar conquered and took possession of Egypt, he was praised and honored by the Romans; had he instead roughed up a few people in Rome, he might have been damned as a ruffian and thief. When Alexander conquered the Near East, he was not regarded by the West as a gangster; neither was Charlemagne after he had conquered Europe....This method is so effective that the application of violence is a jealously guarded monopoly of the government--as a means of keeping itself in power and enforcing the use of *other* methods of competition in ordinary daily life.[1]

Another method of allocating the ticket would be to put names of the three neighbors who are willing to pay $45 in a hat and draw one name out. Is an *equal chance* really equal for our three individuals? It would be if the intensity of their respective desire (i.e., the value of other goods each of them is willing to sacrifice) for the ticket was exactly the same. But it is not, and it is hardly ever the same. In our case an equal chance discriminates in favor of neighbor 3. His stakes are the smallest.

Suppose that Bill asks himself a perfectly normal question: Could I somehow get more than $45 for my ticket without breaking the law? The answer is yes. At the price of $45, he has something to give that is hard to get. Unable to accept more money for the ticket, Bill can *trade favors*. That is, he can choose to sell the ticket to the neighbor who could do something for him.

A car dealer, a physician, a plumber, an attractive member of the opposite sex, and the person in charge of selling tickets for pro-football games are likely to have more favors to trade than a student, a retiree, a clerk and a motherly widow with three kids. Competition by personal characteristics such as connections, important skills, and beauty are commonly used to allocate goods when price competition is curbed by the government.

---

[1] A. Alchian, and W. Allen, *University Economics* (Belmont: Wadsworth, 1964), pp. 26-7.

In general, the rich and the affluent have more favors to trade than the poor and the underprivileged. Thus, price controls make the poor worse off. At the market price, the poor get little of the good they demand. At the controlled price, the poor can afford to buy more of that good, but are likely to get none. The reason is simple: price controls create shortages of goods. Sellers have incentives to allocate goods that are in short supply (at the controlled price) to those people who can do them favors. And the poor are not likely to have favors to trade.

Another consequence of price controls, and a very serious one, is lack of incentives to maintain long-lived goods such as housing. The owner of an apartment subject to rent controls has incentives to invest the funds that might have been used to maintain the building into a higher-valued asset instead. Lack of "decent" housing units in rent-controlled areas of Chicago, Detroit, New York and other major cities is thus a predictable result of restrictions on private property rights.

RATIONING

Suppose the government wants to eliminate competition based on personal attributes because it works against the interest of those the government wanted to help. A way to achieve this is for the government to issue coupons entitling those who get them to a specific amount of the good that is being rationed. Say everybody over 16 years of age gets a coupon to buy 30 gallons of gasoline per month at a controlled price of 30 cents per gallon. This method of resolving the allocation problem was used in the United States during World War II, and is used in many parts of the world today. In fact, many U.S. legislators favored rationing of gasoline during the oil crisis in the 1970s. Rationing goes further than price controls in restricting the right of ownership. In the case of rationing, the government interferes with both transferability of ownership and exclusivity of ownership.

Let us observe two individuals whose monthly demand for gasoline is given in Table 8-1. Data in the Table are hypothetical but they conform to the law of demand, so we can use them to discuss the expected effects of rationing on the allocation of resources.

The supply of gasoline available to those two individuals per unit of time is 60 gallons. As we know, the quantity of gasoline demanded by A and B at various prices depends on their incomes, driving preferences, the types of cars they choose to buy, and prices of other goods (i.e., the value of that which is given up each time they buy one gallon of gas).

Table 8-1. Rationing

Price per gallon in $	Demand by A	Demand by B
1.00	30	0
.90	40	0
.80	50	10
.70	60	20
.60	70	30
.50	80	40
.40	90	50
.30	100	60
.20	110	70
.10	120	80

The difference between A's and B's demand for gasoline does not necessarily mean that A is a richer person. My neighbor has more wealth than I do but I chose to own a more expensive car and drive more miles per day, while my neighbor spends his money on frequent trips to Europe.

In the absence of governmental interference with the right of ownership and contractual freedom, the price of gasoline would tend toward 80 cents per gallon. At that price, the owner of the gasoline would receive $48 from our two individuals, which is the most the owner can get. Suppose the government decides that the price is not fair to B, but it also wants to avoid price controls because A has lots of favors to trade. The government decides that each person will get a coupon entitling the bearer to 30 gallons of gasoline per unit of time at 60 cents per gallon. The gasoline owner now collects only $36, losing $12 as a result of restrictions on the right of ownership.

At 60 cents per gallon, B gets all the gasoline he wants at that price, and pays $18 to the owner. It happens to be the same amount he would have paid for that much gasoline anyway. At the price of 60 cents, A would like to buy 70 gallons of gasoline but all she gets is 30 gallons. Those 30 gallons are worth as much as $30 to her and she gets them for only $18. Her gain of $12 is exactly equal to the owner's loss. Like price controls, rationing transfers income from those who own goods to those who buy them.

At the price of 60 cents, A wants 70 rather than 30 gallons of gasoline. The shortage is due to price controls. This means that some exchange opportunities that would move resources from lower- to higher-valued uses are left unexploited. We can detect those inefficiencies of price controls and observe how the free market corrects them by assuming that the government allows free exchange of coupons, as was the case in the United States during World War II.

In that case, A would offer to buy some gasoline from B at a higher price. B would be happy to trade, because at a higher price he prefers less gasoline and more other things. The price of gasoline would tend to rise to 80 cents per gallon. At that price A and B would get the preferred mix of gasoline. B would have 10 gallons of gasoline, which he values at $8, but would pay only $2. A would get 50 gallons, worth $40 to her, but would pay only $34. Rationing (with or without the market for coupons) would take $12 away from the owner of gasoline. An important consequence of rationing is to reduce incentives to invest in the production of goods that are rationed.

Two issues could be raised here--the same issues could have been raised in connection with price controls: What prevailing principle of ethics says that the owner of a good that is rationed (or subject to price controls) must transfer a part of the value of that good to the buyer as a gift? What principle of economics suggests that a reduction in the future rate of production of goods that are being rationed (or subject to price controls) justifies the transfer of income to current buyers of those goods?

MARKET ENTRY RESTRAINTS

If a producer could restrict potential competitors from free access to the market, that producer's profit would be enhanced. It is therefore predictable that some pressure would be brought to bear on the government to close the market to potential entrants. The reasons given for seeking such protection include encouraging innovation, protecting consumers from fly-by-night sellers, avoiding wasteful duplications, protecting workers from cheap imports, safeguarding the public interest, and others. All those reasons are at best a facade of words serving to protect one producer from competition by another.

Whatever the reason given for seeking protection from competition, the effect is always the same: to restrict the right of ownership.

Let us discuss the effects of legal restrictions on private property rights by going back to our VCR example. Table 7-3 is partially reprinted here as Table 8-2. The market price per VCR is $61. C is producing 100 units at the cost of $3,000. His total receipts are $6,100. E is producing 200 VCRs (at the cost of $10,000) and $10,000 worth of other goods. Her total receipts are $22,200. A, B, and D have no interest in entering the market.

Table 8-2. Demand for VCRs

Price in $	Quantity Demanded
141	140
131	160
121	180
111	200
101	220
91	240
81	260
71	280
61	300

Suppose now that E is successful in persuading the government that only she and C should be allowed to produce VCRs. Being the lower-cost producer, C gets a free ride. Whatever happens to the price of VCRs, he would continue to produce 100 units, the maximum he can produce per unit of time, and enjoy greater revenues. Given legal protection from competition by other producers, E has incentives to search for her own best mix of VCRs and other goods. The example in Table 8-2 is merely a teaching device; it captures the essence of human interactions and responses to new knowledge about exchange opportunities. In a world of uncertainty and incomplete knowledge E has no givens to work with.

At the price of $71, E sells 180 units and produces $11,000 worth of other goods. And her total revenue increases from $22,200 to $23,780. At the price of $91, her total revenue from selling 140 units of VCRs and $13,000 worth of other things would be $25,740. Should E try to sell VCRs at $121, her total revenue would go down to $25,680. By trial and error, E would discover a price between $91 and $121.

As E experiments with various prices, she will discover that at a higher price more competitors (D at $71, B at $91, and so on) begin putting pressure on the government to open the market. Given their subjective perceptions of their influence on the government vis-à-vis their competitors, C and E might trade some profit from higher prices for more security from competition at lower prices. Suppose they choose the price of $91 per VCR. At that price E's total profits would increase from $2,200 in the competitive market ($61 per VCR) to $5,740 in the restricted market ($91 per VCR).

At the price of $91 per VCR and the demand for 240 units, the value of the marginal unit of that good exceeds its costs of production ($50). However, the community is not going to get additional VCRs because restrictions on the right of ownership eliminate a credible threat from producers whose costs of production are less than $91 per VCR.

It appears that the right to be protected from competition is a property right that has money value. The value of this right is the difference between competitive and protected earnings. We expect to observe that the difference is shared by producers (C and E in our case), lobbyists they hire to help them close the market, and government officials who receive campaign contributions to keep the market closed.

RESTRICTIONS ON OPEN MARKETS FOR LABOR

The purpose of minimum wage laws is that everybody should make at least a decent living wage. Unfortunately, there is always a gap between the intent and the observed consequences of exogenous changes in the rules of the game.

Minimum wage laws restrict the worker's property right to seek exchange opportunities for labor below some price determined and enforced by the government. By prohibiting producers from paying their employees less than the legal minimum wage per hour, these laws create unemployment among those individuals whose productivity is below that price; that is, the least skilled workers. Evidence is conclusive that minimum wage laws, like all other forms of price control, tend to hurt precisely those they are supposed to help

The hardest hit groups are teenagers, African Americans, and the aged. Minimum wage laws create incentives for unemployed workers to seek "contracts across markets." If my productivity from driving a taxi is less than the minimum wage, I might rent a cab from the company for a fixed lump sum of money. The money I pay the company equals the company's perceived opportunity costs from using the car elsewhere or selling it. I keep the residual, which is expected to be less than the minimum wage.

Another example of restrictions on the open market for labor is equal pay for equal work. Equal pay for equal work is supposed to reduce discrimination between various classes of employees. It surely sounds fine to take a position that one's personal taste for one class of people over another should be somehow eliminated, even though it may require legal interference with the freedom of voluntary exchange. However, an important question is why and how the market tolerates unequal pay for equal work? It is difficult to imagine that profit-seeking individuals are not going to bid for the services of those who are doing the same work for less remuneration than others. And it is even more difficult to imagine that an increase in the demand for the labor services of the group discriminated against would not increase their earnings. To say that things do not happen that way in a private property, free-market economy is to deny self-interest as a major motivating force.

Suppose a young lawyer, who has just passed the bar exam, is much better able to represent clients successfully than many established lawyers. A high school girl living a few blocks away might be a more reliable baby-sitter than most college girls. A student looking for a summer job might be better at painting houses than are most professional painters. However, they all face the same problem. Information about their relative abilities is not a free good. Potential legal clients, parents with small children, and people who want their homes painted know that on average established lawyers win more cases than new lawyers, that college girls are more reliable than high school girls, and that professional painters know their job better than students looking for temporary work. Those are observed averages that might have little bearing on the performance of a specific person, as in the cases mentioned above.

Yet those observed averages form subjective perceptions on the basis of which people make decisions. At the same rate of pay, clients would prefer an established lawyer, parents would prefer a college girl, and a homeowner would prefer a professional painter. And they could all discover, after the fact, that they could have done better. But the cost of information about people who have not been around to prove their worth is high. How could those individuals lower the cost of information about their respective abilities? They could advertise but why should they be believed? Or they could offer to work for less, by as much less as necessary, in order to compensate their employers for the perceived differences in their abilities vis-à-vis those of more established competitors. As they prove themselves on the job, the knowledge-creating competitive process will open up opportunities for them to get more money for their work.

But they must be free to work for less. Thus, laws requiring equal pay for equal work could only hurt their chances to prove themselves in competitive markets. On the other hand, established lawyers, college girls and professional painters have incentives either to support such laws or to push for union wages.

NOT-FOR-PROFIT ORGANIZATIONS

Not-for-profit firms are organizations in which property rights have two major characteristics. First, their assets are not transferable. Second, they have to spend the residual (i.e., the difference between their revenues and the cost of operations) to further their specific purposes. Examples of not-for-profit property organizations are private colleges, foundations, nonproprietary hospitals, fraternal organizations and churches, among others.

The absence of transferable rights in assets held by not-for-profit organizations means that no one has the right in the residual they (could) produce. An implication is that decision makers in not-for-profit firms do not have incentives to seek the highest-valued uses for assets held by their organizations. What are then decision makers' incentives in not-for-profit institutions?

To address that issue we return to our football example in chapter seven. Why did we observe a shortage of tickets? Why didn't the school try to sell tickets at market-clearing prices? Why didn't the superintendent or the school board fire the manager for failing to do that?

High schools and their athletic departments are not-for-profit organizations. The salary of athletic department's director is not related to his contribution to the firm's residual. Thus, he gains little from "discovering" market clearing prices and selling tickets at those prices. Could he increase his total income without breaking the law?

Given the prevailing property rights in assets held by the firm, the director (or the manager in charge of selling tickets) has incentives to seek other avenues for raising his total compensation. He has two avenues available. The director could trade favors or purchase non-pecuniary goods. For example, he could choose to sell tickets, and especially tickets for the choice seats, below their market-clearing prices. By doing that he creates a shortage of choice seats. Now, the director has something to give that is both inexpensive and unavailable. He would be invited to parties, offered memberships in social clubs, treated to lavish meals, and so on.

Or the director/manager could sell tickets at their market-clearing prices and then proceed to spend lots of money on business trips, entertainment, a plush office, pleasant and congenial co-workers, and other non pecuniary goods that yield satisfaction to him. Expenditures for those goods are reported as the costs of doing business. Perhaps we can now understand why the school did not insist on selling tickets at market clearing prices.

The absence of transferable rights in assets held by not-for-profit firms (i.e., the absence of the right to capture the residual) has two general consequences. First, the performance of not-for-profit firms escapes the scrutiny of financial markets. Thus, the transaction costs of monitoring the behavior of the director and his staff have to be high. Second, no one, except the Internal Revenue Service, has strong incentives to incur the transaction costs of monitoring expenditures by not-for-profit firms--especially, if the director of such a firm routinely invites members of the firm's board of directors and local civic leaders to join him on various working trips.

SUGGESTED READING

K. Brunner, "The Limits of Economic Policy," in *Socialism: Institutional, Philosophical and Economic Issues*, S. Pejovich, ed. (Dordrecht: Kluwer Academic Publishers, 1990).

P. McAvoy, *Regulated Industries and the Economy* (New York: Norton, 1979).

G. Stigler, "The Extent of the Market," *Journal of Law and Economics* 28 (1985).

Chapter 9

FREE-MARKET ECONOMIES, THE STATE, AND POLICY-MAKING

Enrico Colombatto[*]

According to the free-market ideal economic agents should be free to exchange resources, goods and services in order to maximize their objectives--personal satisfaction as consumers and owners of production factors, profits as producers. To this purpose, agents generate and exchange information. They create suitable institutional arrangements in order to ease interaction, to assign, protect and trade property rights; and they also agree on transferring some authority to government bodies, at a local or at a national level. In a free-market system, however, the object of the transfer is authority, not power. Accordingly, the individuals act as principals, whereas those to whom authority is transferred--and can exercise such authority within the geographical and/or functional limits imposed by the principals--are the agents. In a free-market framework agents are therefore responsible to their principals; in particular, agents can be removed, and the realm of their authority can be modified. And when the principal-agent relationship becomes blurred, the free-market economy slides towards the mixed-economy pattern, or towards the command-economy model.

Surely, the result of all these activities is not a Nirvana economy. That is, it is not a situation where everybody behaves in the most efficient way by using all the information available, so that resources are allocated to their most productive uses in a world with no transaction costs, where everything can be predicted with great ease, and uncertainty eliminated. In fact, acquiring and storing information is expensive, and agents may not be willing to produce and process all the data which would be necessary to take a perfectly informed decision. Externalities cannot always be fully internalized.

---

[*] Professor of Economics at the University of Turin, and Director of the International Centre for Economic Research in Turin.

The ownership of property rights may be expensive to enforce or to exchange, so that otherwise desirable transactions do not take place. Moreover, risk and uncertainty remain a permanent feature of the economic life of an individual and of a society as a whole. More generally, uncertainty is an intrinsic feature of innovation, which follows from the people's efforts to better their condition. The very fact that innovation occurs implies that operators expect products and processes in the future to be different from today. The new products and processes available in the future are obviously unknown (uncertain). Hence, from this point of view, the presence of uncertainty is indeed desirable, for it witnesses the presence of fast technological process, of a vital and rapidly growing economic context.

From the above one may perhaps derive the impression that a free-market economy is some kind of a second best, after Nirvana. This would be wrong. Although Nirvana represents a static optimum by definition, it would be clearly sub-optimal in a dynamic context. In fact, in a Nirvana state of the world there would exist very little incentive to improve, to create new products and to experiment new processes. Scarcity would no longer be relevant, growth would become impossible. It would be the end of economics, but economic problems (such as scarcity and the quest for better living conditions) would still be with us. And that would be hardly desirable.

A free-market economy should not be confused with the long run version of the Nirvana state, either. For a free-market economy tends to a long-run competitive equilibrium, but never reaches it, unlike its Nirvana benchmark paradigm. This is due to the innumerable imperfections which make the difference between the textbook version of perfect competition and the real world. And also to the features of such equilibrium, which change continuously, so that the adjustment process never ends. Indeed, such never-ending and imperfect adjustment process is at the very heart of growth. It encourages agents to innovate and improve their decision-making process in order to reduce the scarcity constraints and the cost of those very imperfections (frictions and sources of inefficiencies); and it rewards their efforts.

IMPERFECTIONS, RULE OF LAW, AND BEYOND

There is now widespread agreement on the fact that a free-market economy is still the best of all possible worlds (including Nirvana), for it creates opportunities to innovate and improve welfare, both for the individual and from a public-interest point of view. Hence, individuals are thought to be the obvious candidates to take the decisions which affect their own well-being. It follows that property rights should be defined and assigned to the individual, who should then be free to exchange them, and enforced.

In addition, "free" citizens are deemed capable of generating the appropriate institutional arrangements to enhance suitable interaction, either directly among themselves through informal rules, or through the intermediation of a public body. In a free-market system there is no need to impose from above - possibly by relatively modest majorities of voters - some wiser and almost omniscient agent to tell people what do, and perhaps force them to do it, allegedly for their own good. If such an entity is actually useful, the population will create it spontaneously, and provide it with the authority which is deemed adequate for the purpose.

This certainly applies to monitoring and enforcing the property-right system, a task which the public agent usually fulfills more efficiently than an individual or a group of individuals. But government intervention can also extend beyond monitoring. In particular, government intervention may be considered suitable in order to provide given sets of goods and services, or to solve a wide range of collective-action problems, whereby desirable outcomes could not obtain otherwise. For instance, individuals' behavior may be distorted by informed guesses about other individuals' actions. Some operators may thus decide not to take action unless others do, even if their action would have made everybody in the community better off. Similarly, some sets of individuals may decide that there are ways to contribute to the costs for an amount which corresponds to less than their share of the benefits; once again, sub-optimal outcomes are often the consequence. Under such circumstances, governments[1] may thus become responsible for policy making, both in the domain of

---

[1] Albert Breton has recently pointed out that it would be wrong to consider "government" as one monolithic structure; rather, there are many layers of governmental authority, to which authority can be delegated. That explains the use of the term "governments" in this context.

production (directly or indirectly, through regulation), and of income redistribution.

Yet, some authors would argue that public authorities (governments) should only provide "rule-of-law", that is the rules of the game according to which actors can operate freely. In their view, a policy-making role for governments is not compatible with a role of pure agent.

Of course this raises a crucial question as regards the possibility of having policies in a free-market system. And it explains why the remaining sections of this chapter are devoted to such a very basic issue. Indeed, the difference between the authority to monitor and the authority to decide is critical in this context. The former--called rule-of-law--refers to the monitoring and effective enforcement of the property-right system; the latter--henceforth policy making--refers to the possibility of creating new rules, supposedly in the public interest.[1] In principle, both categories of authority are compatible with a free-market system, as long as government intervention is based on "authority", rather than "power"; i.e. as long as government officials operate as pure agents, and the so-called "private sector" is acknowledged to be the principal. It will be argued, however, that this principal-agent requirement is most likely to be violated in practice.

ON THE ROLE OF GOVERNMENTS

In this light, it is apparent that the debate on the role of governments in a free-market economy revolves around three broad categories of topics: (1) the evaluation of the features which legitimize the transfer of authority from the realm of individual decision-making to government; (2) the analysis of the incentive systems to which government behavior responds, that is the extent to which the civil servant's personal goals depend on his ability to deliver in the public interest; and (3) the birth and evolution of the institutional frameworks.

Of course, such topics are closely related. If the transfer is not legitimate, the substance of the transfer is not only authority, but includes power as well. Under such circumstances the principles of a

---

[1] This distinction is the same as that put forward in J. Buchanan and G. Tullock, *The Calculus of Consent, Logical Foundations of Constitutional Democracy* (Ann Arbor: University of Michigan Press, 1962).

free-market society would thus be undermined, since property rights would not be the object of a voluntary exchange, but rather of arbitrary extortion carried out by a more or less qualified majority. In addition, the rules which affect the creation and development of a society are influenced by how much power is attributed to the institutional actors. If such actors have only authority, but no power, then institutions adapt to the needs of a free society and the state limits the production of goods and services to those areas where it is more efficient. Should agents prove unable to adjust, then the public body would lose authority - either agents are replaced, or the unsatisfactory set of norm is canceled. But if agents have at least some power, and therefore are not entirely dependent on the public, then officials will be able to take advantage of their power in order to pursue their own personal interests, and even to change the rules of the game so as to expand their rent-seeking opportunities.

This insight can easily lead to extreme views. On the one hand, it is argued that unless some kind of a Wicksellian rule holds--i.e., unanimity or quasi-unanimity for constitutional law-making--governments are bound to develop their own interests, make it difficult for the principal(s) to control them, and eventually become some kind of rent-seeking leviathans living at the expense of the community. Put differently, it would be impossible to imagine a rule-of-law function for government, for it would be just the first step towards "unauthorized" policy making. Contrary to this view, it has been maintained that governments in fact compete among themselves, and are subject to an effective system of check and balances, so that their role is by and large consistent with the desires of the population. Hence, they are efficient, that is they are welfare maximizing; and they may well be required to redistribute income and/or produce services and commodities, if in the public interest. From this standpoint, there would be no need to analyze what the role of government should be; just as it would made little sense to discuss about what and how much a firm should produce in a competitive environment.

If the former view is accepted, and given that consent on rule-of-law is usually based on a qualified majority at most, then governments should be denied any role, for they would interfere with private economic activities, expand rent-seeking and thwart opportunities for growth. This we call the traditional (normative) *laissez-faire* illusion. At the other extreme, the check-and-balances belief supports virtually any role for government, both in the rule-of-law and in the policy-making domains. Short-time imbalances remain possible, of course; but the check-and-balances system makes sure that the median voter forces the public body to pursue the most efficient outcomes, in order to preserve its authority. This we call the neo-classical myth of institutional engineering, which is derived from a positive interpretation of the *laissez-faire* dogma.

FROM THE NORMATIVE *LAISSEZ-FAIRE* FALLACY...

The "no-government" hypothesis is usually known as *laissez-faire*. It has not much to do with the free-market notion, although it is undeniable that both the *laissez-faire* and free market ideas share a deep mistrust towards the role of the state as producer of private goods, and an almost equally deep fear of the state as the instrument to carry out income redistribution. But that is where the similarity ends.

Indeed, the *laissez-faire* misconception is one of the major threats to the notion of a free-market economy[1]. In contrast with a free-market framework, the *laissez-faire* dogma denies all kinds of role for the state. This is not just theory, of course; for there are plenty of (undeveloped) countries where the state does not exist. The consequences of such a regime are however hardly desirable, for in a world with no rules all agents tend to behave as short-term bandits. Uncertainty dominates, and the resources required to reduce it--even in the very short run--leave very little for productive activities. In other words, a *laissez-faire* situation is characterized by anarchy, rather than by freedom; at least until some informal institutional arrangement emerges. Obviously, there is little room for a market to develop in the meantime. In most cases, an autocrat will eventually take power. *Laissez-faire* will thus be more likely to persist under a totalitarian regime, where the autocrat nullifies spontaneous attempts to reduce uncertainty through contracts, and thus makes the allocation of property rights inefficient.

The empirical evidence is by and large consistent with such a prediction. An economy usually develops more easily in a democracy, where the opposition to rule-of-law is weaker; while widespread poverty tends to persist under totalitarian regimes, which of course

---

[1] See F. Hayek, *The Road to Serfdom* (London: Routledge, Kegan and Paul, 1979 edition), p.13.

tend to favor anarchy, and where violence is routine. In particular, it is apparent that a free economy is not compatible with the *laissez-faire* model, since in the latter property rights are breached systematically by means of violence. And of course there can be no freedom without property rights.

Yet, although the normative value of the *laissez-faire* dogma is now considered unacceptable in virtually all quarters, it still survives. It is popular among those who fail to perceive the difference between anarchy and free market, and refer to the former in order to discredit the latter. It is also important, and perhaps a little more useful, as a benchmark in order to evaluate and compare different institutional systems.

... TO POSITIVE *LAISSEZ-FAIRE* AND SOCIAL ENGINEERING

Although the economic profession does not give any credit to its normative implications, a substantial number of authoritative scholars has been considering *laissez-faire* a methodological guideline in order to formulate positive assessments about how an economy works in a democracy. This is the current neo-classical interpretation of *laissez-faire*, whereby agents are no longer left to themselves in an institutional vacuum, but are assumed to operate in a democracy. Within this framework, the positive interpretation of the *laissez-faire* tenet maintains that all the institutional arrangements which characterize a democratic country are going to be efficient, for they are generated by the interaction of the market and electoral forces, until an equilibrium solution is reached, whereby the marginal benefits of government intervention equal marginal costs.

As a consequence, the neo-classical view of how a free-market economy operates rejects the traditional version of *laissez-faire*, which is critical of all government policies. Instead, it accepts a positive version which is against any attempt aimed at tampering with the role of governments, which in turn is supposed to be the result of a democratic decision-making process. Governments are thus deemed to be the outcome of a competitive process whereby agents buy desirable goods (or services) and equalize the marginal costs of providing government services and the marginal benefits of such services.

Positive *laissez-faire* often leads to social and institutional engineering. This can be explained by observing that success in reaching a desirable competitive-equilibrium solution in ordinary law-making depends crucially on the nature of the interaction among agents, which is disciplined by constitutional arrangements. Thus, the neo-classical approach holds that if the constitutional framework is "adequate", market failures cannot persist. The political market typical of democracy would always provide a suitable government solution. And agents would for instance agree on transferring production--or assigning new regulating powers--to government authorities. Or they would take such authority away, or perhaps move it from one government to another.

It then follows that if the political market is not able to generate suitable solutions to a market-failure problem, intervention is required in order to remove the impediments to a smooth functioning of the democratic decision-making process, and solve all possible collective-action problems quickly enough. Constitutional engineering is thus needed in order to create or restore a satisfactory institutional environment, or just to speed up institutional change. In the long run, however, constitutional changes are assumed to occur spontaneously, as long as agents are able to interact, and influence the law-making process according to their expected flows of cost and benefits.

This comes very close to violating "rule-of-law", though. For according to the positive *laissez faire* approach the traditional collective-action problems are eliminated by the fact that the strength of the coalition supporting or opposing constitutional change reflects the cost and benefits of such change. If so, the outcome would be efficient, but at the same time it would eliminate the need for a Wicksellian majority, or indeed for a majority altogether. Social engineering would follow, since individuals could be deprived from their property rights by more or less qualified majorities, the action of which is justified by their very intensity, rather than by their legitimacy.

This approach raises a vast number of other issues - spanning from economics to ethics, to political science - which cannot be covered adequately in these pages. All of them, however, focus on the one basic point mentioned at the beginning of this chapter. That is, on our understanding of the way a free-market economy works and, in particular, of how institutional frameworks created in a democratic environment may enhance or hinder its activity.

THE IMPOSSIBILITY OF THE FREE-MARKET

As has been pointed out earlier on, a free-market economy exists and produces its benefits only within a formal and/or informal, fairly complete, institutional framework. A reasonably precise and known system of rules and sanctions allows agents to maximize their welfare by taking into account the possibility of interacting with other actors (specialization by product and by process) and by extending their objective into the future (investment). In addition, it is essential that some authority is transferred to a public body, to be made responsible for the enforcement of rule-of-law. An inefficient public body is still much more desirable than private solutions. Similar comments may also apply to policy-making functions. In both cases, however, a free-market economy remains such only if individuals maintain full control of power.

The rule-of-law problem

Let us now focus on rule-of-law. This term refers to the important but rather limited number of areas where the provision of services by government corresponds to situations similar to natural monopoly, and, more generally, enforcement of property rights. Education may be included, too. Not because governments have a natural monopoly in this area, but rather because children and adolescents may suffer from the choices of their parents as regards the amount and the quality of schooling they would buy. In all these cases a public authority is usually thought to perform more efficiently than individuals. In particular, it is assumed to be preferable, as long as it broadly suits the needs of the public interest, and does not exceed in taking advantage of the monopoly power and thus in extracting rents. One can therefore think of a trade-off between the inefficiencies and rent-seeking activities associated with government, which is protected by a legal monopoly and draws legitimacy from the electorate[1]; and the inefficiencies associated with a private monopolist, who might be

---

[1] The greater the degree of legitimacy, the vagueness about the terms of the authority transfer, and the uncertainty of the private-monopoly option, the larger the amount of inefficiency and rent-seeking carried out by governments. For an application to the history of trade policy see D. Verdier, *Democracy and International Trade* (Princeton: Princeton University Press, 1994).

tempted to exploit his current monopoly on the use of violence (defense, law and order) in order to maximize rent-seeking and rent-extraction.

Of course, incumbent politicians and top bureaucrats realize that their inefficiencies and rent-seeking activities may give birth to opposition, so that their prospects for long-term office are jeopardized. Actually, some time after inception, opposition emerges anyway, since at least some of the principals are going to be unhappy about the original rule-of-law framework, either because the existing framework is not thought to be enforced satisfactorily, or because the constitutional framework is thought to need revision. This is almost inevitable, since *ex-ante* uncertainty and fear of normative *laissez-faire* usually induces some principals not to oppose the birth of a given set of "initial" institutions. That is, lack of information about the cause-effect mechanisms associated with them, about the practical details of enforcement, and about civil servants' misbehavior often induces principals to accept constitutional arrangements which anyway allow them to escape the normative-*laissez-faire* trap. All this makes sure that the necessary majority is acquired, so that the initial institutional construct sees the light. But of course the very reasons which induced people to accept a sub-optimal institutional arrangement guarantee that sooner or later, at least in some quarters, the desire for change comes to the surface.

Opposition, though likely, is however not enough to deter government officials from shirking and departing from ideal action in pursuit of the public interest. Both because the rules of the game contain a bias which favors the incumbent government actors; And because officials strive to engage in policy making, to transform authority into power.

As regards the first point, the very fact that a qualified-majority rule is usually required to create and/or to change a constitution originates an asymmetry, the relevance of which can hardly be overestimated. The Wicksellian principle is indeed accepted relatively easily at the beginning of a constitutional history, say after a war, or a very major crisis[1]. But it works in reverse gear when a substantial minority or even a not-large-enough majority is unhappy with the existing institutions. The Wicksellian majority is no longer required to

---

[1] See M. Olson, *The Rise and Decline of Nations* (New Haven: Yale University Press, 1982).

legitimize a constitutional framework already in place. Put differently, you need a qualified majority to agree on the initial constitutional arrangement, and such a majority is relatively easy to obtain when the opportunity cost of not reaching an agreement is very high (normative *laissez-faire*). But you also need a qualified majority in order to change such an arrangement, even if it turns out to be unsatisfactory for a fairly large share of the population.

Agents know this, of course, and behave accordingly, in order to weaken their links with the principals, and thus create opportunities for rent-seeking. This last goal is pursued by making sure that the constitutional framework allows that governments be made responsible for some amount of policy-making. As will be made clear shortly, policy making creates more opportunities for rent-seeking, and also makes it easy for agents to collude against their principals. In addition, actors look for legitimacy to their discretionary actions, so that governments end up by using resources to foster their own power, to the detriment of the rest of the population, and blur the line between personal inefficiencies and institutional shortcomings. As has been noted by several authors, even the most neutral constitutional frame is subject to interpretation by those in charge of its enforcement[1].

The "Wicksellian asymmetry" described above is virtually unavoidable, for it stems from the initial quest for stability, at the expense of the need for a flexible institutional arrangement and of a pure principal-agent relation. Thus, it is inevitable that government agents acquire some power, not only authority. As a consequence, free-market principles are violated, and individual property rights are transferred to an extent which goes beyond the level some individuals are willing to agree to. Although governments still draw their legitimacy from the people, the principal-agent link is weakened, and a free-market model is replaced by a mixed economy. Of course, should governments draw legitimacy from other sources than the electorate (say, principles and ideologies), then the shift towards a command economy context would be more likely.

The outcome is well known--distortions and deadweight welfare losses. On the one hand governments are required to use their discretionary power in order to pursue particular gains, rather than the

---

[1] See for instance P. Bernholz, "On the Political Economy of the Transformation of Political and Economic Regimes", *Virginia Political Economy Lecture Series*, Fairfax, Va., 1992.

general interest; on the other, governments use this power and these demands for their own rent-seeking activities.

The policy-making problem

The effect of the Wicksellian asymmetry described above becomes particularly powerful when governments use their rule-of-law power to legitimize policy making. This takes place when Wicksellian majorities legitimize transfers of authority to governments, and non-Wicksellian majorities (or even minorities) allow governments to use such authority in order to acquire power. The exercise of power generates rent-seeking through three channels: pure redistribution (for instance, state pensions financed on the basis of a pay-as-you-go criterion), production (as is the case for state-owned firms), redistribution through production (a typical example is provided by many national health-care programs).[1]

Once again, it is worth emphasizing that in principle policy making is not necessarily in contrast with the free-market ideal. Rather, the crucial constraint is that in a free-market economy such activities must be agreed upon by a Wicksellian majority, which are to decide both on whether such matters must be delegated to government agencies and, if so, on the layer of government which should be made responsible.

Can governments be forced to operate as agents, as the positive *laissez-faire* approach discussed earlier maintains? The answer is "no", both because there exist information and collective-action problems, and because governments behave in a non-competitive way.

When a government agent has authority, he will try to maximize his degrees of freedom on issues of economic relevance, so as to increase his rent-seeking opportunities, possibly in a long-time perspective. Thus, he will try to favor policy-making by means of *ad hoc* interpretation of the constitution, by promoting the formation of simple majorities or strong-enough minorities to support his action or, when necessary, by acting as a simple broker, and thus play one coalition against the other.

---

[1] In fact, the outcome is still a matter of redistribution even in the case of production, since taxpayers are asked to pay for the losses accumulated by inefficient state firms, or consumers are asked to pay a higher price for goods and services produced in a normative-monopoly regime.

This is the core strategy of most redistributive policies, which usually contain two elements. One which plays in favor of the interest groups which have fought in favor of the redistributive bills at the moment of their inception, and tends to decay with time. The other which tends to obfuscate the size and sign of the net flows involved, so that groups become hesitant to galvanize into an effective coalition against redistribution. This result is obtained through substantial increases in public expenditure, regulation, and a large number of different policies aimed at cutting through possible coalitions of losers, leading to fragmentation. The ultimate aim is to make popular drive against policy-making rewarding for everybody only if such a movement regards a major downsizing in overall redistribution. But that would imply that many bills should be canceled more or less simultaneously; that interest-group fragmentation is avoided; and that information costs for the individual fall substantially. These constraints are very difficult to meet. The legislative processes usually allow the examination of one bill at a time, so that time-inconsistency issues prevail. Furthermore, the cost of information tends to rise dramatically when new legislation involves the evaluation of many policy-making programs at the same time, with all the interaction effects. Finally, the uncertain flow of benefits due to a reduction in policy-making are discounted at a much higher rate than the certain flow of costs due to the reduction in subsidies, job security, trade protection, and the like.

In short, public opinion exerts a rather soft constraint on government action in modern democracies. In this light, the similarity and extreme vagueness (if not inconsistency) of the official economic agendas of the various political parties witness the little pressure imposed on them by the electorate; and they also witness the capacity of the policy makers to behave as principals, with enough degrees of freedom to pursue their own personal aims, irrespective of the public interest.

This takes us to second and final point. Governments face weak controls from the electorate, there is no free entry (new agencies are created by the incumbent politicians and rent-seeking groups, not by the candidates to government), and bureaucrats and politicians are fairly mobile among the various layers of governments. Hence, collusion is much more likely to emerge than competition. Federal constitutional frameworks may indeed prevent collusion better than in unitary states. But there is substantial evidence that in the long run collusion takes over, so that Federal governments eventually succeed in subtracting authority and power from the peripheral governments. Put differently, federal constitutions are preferable, for they slow down the slide toward a mixed-economy state. But they are unlikely to keep intact the original principal-agent relation, which makes sure that a free-market economy obtains.

CONCLUDING REMARKS

The analysis of the role of government in a free-market economy put forward in this chapter has shown that it is virtually impossible for an economy to be run according to free-market principles, once individuals decide to transfer some authority to government. Even if such authority is restricted to rule-of-law, the Wicksellian asymmetry makes sure that government "agents" do not bear the cost of not pursuing the public interest through a competitive mechanism. Eventually they manage to get hold of some power, and thus engage in rent-seeking by introducing some elements typical of a mixed economy. Yet, the transfer of authority (and power) to governments is still desirable, for the rule-of-law services provided by governments in democracies are far more efficient than the outcome associated with other solutions; even if that implies the distortions and deadweight welfare losses associated with policy-making and rent-seeking.

It then follows that the free-market system should be considered as benchmark, rather than a realistic possibility. For it is virtually impossible to reach almost unanimity on an institutional framework, unless the alternative is anarchy. And once institutions are there, a path-dependent process sets in, so that the economy slides away from the free-market model, as the transfer of authority becomes transfer of power. Surely, constitutional engineering at the start may help in slowing down the involuntary transfer of power from the individuals to government(s). But the scope for such exercise is more limited than one may imagine, since the initial effort to shape the best possible institutional shell should nevertheless be consistent with the existing set of informal rules, with the widely-accepted customs and standards in use. Failure to meet this consistency requirement would deprive formal rules of legitimacy. The quest for perfect world would weaken rule-of-law and lead to normative *laissez-faire*, anarchy, and possibly totalitarian solutions.

SUGGESTED READINGS

A. Breton, *Competitive Governments an Economic Theory of Politics and Public Finance* (Cambridge: Cambridge University Press, 1996).

B. de Jouvenel, *The Ethics of Redistribution* (Indianapolis: Liberty Fund, 1990).

W. Niskanen, *Bureaucracy and Public Economics* (Cheltenham: Edward Elgar, 1994).

Chapter 10

PROPERTY RIGHTS IN SOCIALISM, EXCHANGE AND PRODUCTION

The system of central economic planning and the labor-managed economy were not ad hoc models invented by and limited to a few countries. They were the consequence of the basic philosophical and economic premises of the socialist doctrine as it has evolved since the eighteenth century (Chapter 6)

The rejection of private property rights was the central premise of socialism from its earliest days, and the abolition of private property rights was the driving ideological force behind all socialist experiments in the twentieth century. To understand the consequences of socialism in a world of uncertainty and incomplete knowledge, we here discuss the basic characteristics of institutional arrangements in the former USSR and the former Yugoslavia and analyze their actual incentives and transaction costs, rather than contemplating the frictionless blackboard model of what Marx meant, what he should have meant, what Lenin and Stalin should have done, or what the Yugoslavs should have done to make the labor-managed economy viable.

THE SYSTEM OF CENTRAL ECONOMIC PLANNING

The term *state ownership* is merely a facade hiding the true owner: whoever controls the state. The major objective of the ruling elite in a socialist state is to strengthen and perpetuate its own power. That is why it is important for the ruling group to control the allocation and use of resources. State ownership in resources gives the ruling elite the right to choose the allocation of resources, the right to determine the distribution of income, and the right to control entry into and exit from the power hierarchy.

In the former Soviet Union, the ruling elite was called the *nomenklatura*. It was about one million strong and divided into several tiers. The top tier included top party leaders, while the lowest consisted of key people in the economy, education, and scientific institutions. The nomenclatura had three sources of wealth. The salary of even a lower-tier nomenklaturist was about ten times the average salary in the USSR. The so-called approved benefits (access to special shops, special restaurants, special hospitals, special resorts, state-owned dachas, etc.) were the second source of wealth. Finally, the benefits tolerated included patronage, good jobs for family members, travel abroad, tickets for entertainment events, and the like. A person would earn all those benefits by being recruited into the ruling group and lose them by being kicked out of it.

The ruling elite's power to pursue its objectives was limited by its perception of the minimum bundle of rights which members of the community expected to have in return for their sacrifice of economic, civic and political freedoms. This bundle of rights was, in effect, the opportunity costs of the people. The following goods figured most prominently during pre-Gorbachev years: guarantee of employment, undemanding work pace, slow but steady rise in living standard, and stable prices.

The relationship between the ruling group and the people could be then treated as the *social contract*, which the people did not choose voluntarily. The power of the ruling group determined the nature of the contract, while the opportunity costs of the people defined its terms (the expected minimum bundle of rights). A change in the contract would be a change in the system, as it happened in 1991. A change in the terms of the contract would have reflected the ruling group's perception of a change in the opportunity costs of the people.

The Mechanism of Economic Planning.

Economic planning means that vertical relations (administrative orders) replace horizontal relations (contracts). Administrative orders flow from the top leadership through various bureaucratic channels down to productive units. The economic plan is in effect the sum total of those orders.

Given the ruling's group preference for the allocation of resources, the distribution of income, and the output mix, the central planning agency in the former Soviet Union and its subordinate units were charged with providing economic and technical solutions for decisions and directives issued by the ruling group. In terms of standard economic theory, the planning bureaucracy had to find a way to keep the economy on the production frontier (the efficiency requirement) and to produce a mix of outputs corresponding to the point on the production frontier chosen by the ruling group (the allocation requirement).

The planning bureaucracy determined production targets for business firms (we can skip the details of the process) on the basis of the past performance of enterprises, new capacities, new priorities, hoped-for changes in productivity, and other indicators. Given their production targets, enterprises had to be able to count on an adequate supply of inputs. However, to have allowed firms to purchase supplies in open markets could easily have modified the plan's objectives and frustrated the will of the ruling elite. Thus, perhaps the most critical part of economic planning included the planning of supplies.

In the former Soviet Union, the bureaucracy controlled the allocation of about 40,000 inputs and the production plans of about 500,000 firms of one kind or another. The allocation of inputs to enterprises, the so-called supply plan, then, was an essential part of the system of central economic planning. Material balances were drawn up for all products--a cumbersome and costly process (again we skip the details). Material balances and production targets were used as the basis for the allocation of inputs to individual enterprises. Several layers of bureaucracy were involved in the process of making, monitoring, and enforcing the supply plan.

The problem in this system is that even a small deviation from the supply plan must cause a chain reaction throughout the system. Suppose the firms producing screws and bolts failed to deliver them on time to other firms. The rate of output at firms awaiting the hardware would fall. Next, enterprises that depended on those firms' outputs would be affected. And so on. To make adjustments and revisions of the plan possible, the ruling group had to design low- and high-priority areas, and then use administrative orders to shift resources from the former into the latter. In the former USSR, low-priority areas were agriculture, services and consumer goods.

The essence of central economic planning in the Soviet Union and most East European countries was the flow of information up the bureaucratic ladder and the flow of orders down to the bottom of the bureaucratic hierarchy: the firm. In a centrally planned economy goods are not bought and sold; they are delivered. In comparison, state-owned firms in capitalist economies are also subject to numerous restrictions and are given their budgets, but they purchase supplies in the market.

Transaction Costs in a Centrally Planned Economy

The absence of market signals in a planned economy makes for high transaction costs of deciding who should do what, preparing the plan, and checking the reports by subordinate units for accuracy--much higher than in a private property economy. Subordinate units in the system of economic planning have strong incentives to maintain and enhance the transaction costs of monitoring their performance.

Transaction costs specific to the system of central economic planning are the value of human and nonhuman resources needed to (1) enforce the plan (by suppressing the process of bidding for goods, the ruling elite deprives the economy of a low-cost method of determining the value of resources in alternative uses); (2) prepare the economic plan; (3) maintain and protect the rules of the game (compare the size of armed forces, the role of security forces, or the number of political prisoners in socialist and capitalist countries); and (4) prevent managers of business firms and lower administrative agencies from falsifying their reports to superiors.

Given the staggering cost of information about the available supplies of resources, alternative production techniques, and the capabilities of the existing firms, economic planners needed a stable relationship between monetary and real magnitudes. For that reason, most prices and the minimum supply of money needed for carrying out real transactions specified in the plan were subject to strict administrative controls. Business firms were not allowed to keep cash balances (those could support nonplanned transactions) and they had to make all payments to other firms and agencies by transferring budgeted balances from one account to another.

Spontaneous Development of Informal Channels of Influence

While the common objective of the top leaders in centrally planned economies is to preserve and enhance the prevailing institutional structure, members of the leadership have strong incentives to seek ways to enhance their own positions *within* the group. Those incentives include being alert to internal alliances within the upper echelon of leadership and appointments (and promotions) of friends to important posts in the ruling elite. The consequences of those incentives were quite similar in all socialist economies, including Yugoslavia.

Pursuing incentives based on the marriage of political power and economic wealth (a major consequence of state ownership), members of the top leadership in all socialist states created their personal "courts." Then, pursuing the same set of incentives, members of the court gathered around each top leader formed their own courts, and so on. In this manner, informal channels of influence developed in socialist economies.

Predictably, those courts were in competition with one another for power and influence. An implication of the existence of such competing channels of influence in socialist states was that their bureaucracies became less concerned about the substance of policies handed down by the bureaucratic hierarchy, and more interested in discovering who made them and who was pushing them. Reaction to policies was then affected by the balance of power between competing courts. Ministries, industries and enterprises sought changes in their administrative orders through their own or a friendly court. Informal channels also created a market for "insiders" who traded on information about issues debated at the higher levels of government.

This informal political structure explains the "purges" in all socialist countries. Whenever a member of the top leadership died or was ejected from power, members of that leader's court were quickly retired, too. Since Stalin frequently changed the composition of the politburo, he had to purge a larger number of people than his successors. A top Soviet spy explained the working of those courts in gruesome detail.[1]

TWO ATTEMPTS TO SAVE SOCIALISM

Perestroika

The purpose of perestroika in the late 1980s was to save the Soviet system by adjusting the terms of the social contract to perceived

---

[1] P. Sudoplatov and A. Sudoplatov, *Special Tasks*, (Boston: Little Brown and Company, 1994), pp. 292-317.

changes in the opportunity costs of the people. Changes in the latter boiled down to a simple proposition: the present value of the costs of *building* socialism increased relative to people's perceptions of the present value of promised benefits.

Gorbachev's perestroika is an excellent example of how misleading neoclassical economics could be in discussing institutional restructuring. A review of literature from the late 1980s would show that the focus of discussion was on the consequences of perestroika rather than on the institutional changes that perestroika required.

Perestroika addressed three critical problems of the system of central economic planning: how to make firms more efficient, how to reduce shortages, and how to curb the power of the bureaucracy.

Efficiency of Firms

In a centrally planned economy, the ruling elite allocates capital goods to business firms, transfers existing capital goods from one enterprise to another, and decides what to do with investment funds. The firm cannot sell, rent, or modify capital goods in its possession. It can only use them to produce (and overproduce) its prescribed output target. Since the firm pays no rent for the use of capital goods, the manager considers capital goods to be a free reserve. There is no penalty for having too much capital (relative to the firm's output target), and the excess capital comes in handy for breakdowns and emergencies. The manager of a centrally planned firm has incentives to press administrative superiors for more capital.

By making the Soviet manager's rewards depend on the firm's profitability (defined as the ratio of profits to the stock of capital), the ruling elite was hoping to influence managerial behavior through turning accumulated reserves of capital into a liability. However, to make the Soviet manager cost-oriented and interested in minimizing holdings of capital, the prevailing property rights in capital goods had to change. The ruling elite had to give the manager the right to control not only the firm's replacement capital but also new additions to the firm's stock of capital; that is, the mix of output produced by capital goods industries. But to grant the manager this right, the ruling elite had to give up its own right of controlling output produced by capital goods industries. The choice was to leave the Soviet manager frustrated in pursuing the new incentives.

Shortages

Perestroika proposed to deal with the shortage of supplies by allowing business enterprises to negotiate contracts with each other. Free contracting for supplies meant that voluntary horizontal relations among enterprises would replace vertical administrative orders. To make this reform operational, the ruling elite had to transfer two property rights from itself to the firm. First, because the output of one firm is the supply of inputs for another, the Soviet manager had to have the right to decide who to produce for and by implication how much to produce. Second, the implementation of free contracting requires competitive markets and scarcity prices (so that managers could know the opportunity costs of the inputs used by their firms). The ruling elite never got around to transferring those property rights to business enterprises.

Bureaucratic Power

Predictably, perestroika had few friends in the Soviet ruling elite, especially within the middle and lower echelons. From their standpoint, the only relevant costs of perestroika were those borne by themselves. And the relevant cost of any specific institutional change had to be the effect of that change on the power and privileges of a cluster of nomenklaturists. Given the principal-agent costs of monitoring the nomenklatura, and uncertainty about the opportunity costs of the people, Gorbachev had to make some difficult choices. He had to assume either that the opportunity costs of the people had risen to outstrip the cost of perestroika to the nomenklatura, or that the costs borne by the nomenklatura were greater than the opportunity costs of the people. It appears that Gorbachev couldn't decide which way to go and shifted his position on several occasions until he was, in effect, overthrown by both groups.

The Labor-Managed Economy

When Stalin threw Yugoslavia out of the Soviet bloc in 1948, the Yugoslav economic system was a carbon copy of the Soviet-type economy, with all the economic and political problems of that system.

In the pursuit of its survival, Tito's clique had to open up the economy to trade with the West. To accomplish that objective, the Yugoslav ruling elite embarked on a series of institutional restructuring subject to two major constraints that were to remain in force until Tito's death in 1980: state ownership of enterprises, and political monopoly of the ruling group. Within those two constraints, institutional changes in Yugoslavia were frequent and uneven.

In late 1949, the three top communist leaders Djilas, Kardelj and Kidric, literally during discussion in a parked car, came up with the idea of the labor-managed economy. They sold the idea to a reluctant Tito and by mid-1950 the Yugoslav labor-managed economy was born.

The turning point in Yugoslavia's departure from the system of central economic planning was the 1950 passage of the Law on Management of Enterprises by Workers' Collectives. The 1951 Law on the Management of Capital Goods by Enterprises clarified the issue of handling the firm's assets, by giving workers' councils a *sui generis* property right over the firm's nonhuman assets: the right of use. The firm was allowed to sell its assets to other firms and to change the composition of its assets. However, the firm also had to maintain the value of its assets via depreciation allowances and reinvestment of the proceeds from sale of capital goods. The Law of Banks of 1961 started a long, and perhaps the most difficult, process in the development of the labor-managed economy: the search for a method of allocating investment funds in an environment in which the ruling group has the right of ownership in capital goods, while the working collective has the right to appropriate the flow of returns from those assets. The labor-managed economy of Yugoslavia continued to evolve throughout the 1960s and early 1970s. Economic planning was abolished, but not the monopoly power of the party.

The labor-managed economy in the former Yugoslavia is the only labor-managed economy that has ever been tried on such a large scale. Its major institutional features were: (1) state ownership of capital goods, (2) the employees' ownership of the returns from capital goods, (3) the employees' right to govern the firm, (4) the substitution of bank credit for the system of administrative distribution of investable funds, and (5) the system of quasi-contracts between all economic agents.

Disappointed with the performance of the Soviet-type economy, critics of capitalism saw the labor-managed economy as a long hoped-for alternative to capitalism. Workers' participation in decision making satisfied an important emotional need, while state ownership in capital assets of business assured the critics of capitalism that the socialist character of the system is being preserved. Nor surprisingly, by the mid-1960s, the Yugoslav system of labor participation in the management of enterprises had captured worldwide attention.

By ignoring the fact that the labor-managed economy did not emerge spontaneously, the supporters of the labor-managed economy ignored incentives and transaction costs specific to the system. Thus, blame for the subsequent failure of the labor-managed economy was put at the door of the political monopoly of the party and its bureaucracy. The question of whether the labor-managed economy (invented and imposed by the party) could have survived without the party's political monopoly was ignored.

The (general) labor-managed firm with its incentives and transaction costs is discussed in some detail in chapter fourteen

SOCIALISM, CAPITALISM, AND THE CONSUMER

The purpose of this section is to provide a summary of the consequences of socialism and capitalism on the well-being of individuals in the community.

Suppose that people in capitalist city of Denver decide, for whatever reason, to drink more California wine. As the demand for wine per unit of time increases, wine stores in Denver discover that their inventories of California wine are being depleted. Driven by desire for more wealth, the owners of wine stores increase their weekly orders of California wine from warehouses. As they try to fill those new orders, the owners of warehouses would discover that their inventories of California wine are also being depleted--nobody is asking for less of it. So they order more wine from California. However, wine producers in California may not be able to satisfy their increased demand for wine immediately. Their inventories are limited, too.

Whether warehouses serving wine stores in Denver offer to pay more for additional quantities of wine per unit of time, or wine producers inform those warehouses that they have to pay more money per gallon of wine, the price of California wine is going to be bid up for all consumers. People whose demand for California wine has not changed are then going to buy less California wine at a higher price. And the amount of California wine they release is the amount of additional wine that people whose demand for California wine has increased are going to get. As the price of California wine goes up, people in Denver would still demand more California wine but not as much as they demanded at the old price.

An increase in the price of California wine then serves two critical allocative functions in a private property, free-market society. It moves some of the good (in our case California wine) from individuals whose demand has not changed to individuals whose demand has increased. And at a higher price for wine, new resources will be reallocated by their owners from lower-valued uses to the wine industry.

Suppose now that the same situation occurs in a socialist city of Kiev. As the demand for Georgia wine per unit of time increases in Kiev, wine stores discover that queues for wine are getting longer. The managers of wine stores are legally responsible for passing that information to an administrative superior, who is likewise legally responsible for informing another administrative superior. Information about a change in the demand for Georgia wine in Kiev then travels up the planning hierarchy.

While in a private property economy information about a change in the demand for any good has the force of a command, the socialist bureaucracy may or may not respond to a change in the demand for any good. There is no built-in incentive for bureaucrats to do so.

Not having the choice of satisfying their desire for more Georgia wine by offering to pay more (and having wine transferred to them from those whose demand has not changed), people in Kiev must either get to wine stores earlier in order to get a good place in the queue, or find a way to trade favors with a store manager. Price controls or not, the price of wine in Kiev would go up in a way that is arbitrary and associated with high transaction costs.

SUGGESTED READING

O. Ioffe, and P. Maggs, *The Soviet Economic System: A Legal Analysis* (Boulder: Westview press, 1987).

G. Warren Nutter, *Political Economy and Freedom, A Collection of Essays* (Indianapolis: Liberty Press 1983).

S. Pejovich, S. "A Property Rights Analysis of the Yugoslav Miracle," *Annals of the American Academy of Political Science,* 1990.

solved long ago. In fact, this approach misses a fundamental point. In the absence of a major shock that destroys existing rent-seeking coalitions, transition towards a free-market regimes is feasible only if the incumbent rent-seekers are compensated or protected. Trade policy often serves this purpose, so that trade flows and capital movements are usually the last and more difficult areas to liberalize. Therefore, the crucial question is not "how good is free trade", but rather "how far can pro-trade coalitions go in the law-bargaining game against protectionist lobbies".

At the other extreme, the structuralist view holds that government should maintain protectionist trade policies in order to compensate for market failures. But the structuralist view doesn't explain why there exist significant market failures in the first place. Indeed, it is not surprising that structuralist recipes on trade usually end up by strengthening those very groups who are content with the prevailing state of affairs. And in practice, structuralist strategies generally allow incumbent dominant interest groups to entrench their position; and the hoped for development never seems to occur. It therefore appears that the traditional approaches address a relevant issue,. But tend to raise wrong questions. As a result, they fail to assess whether--and to what extent--trade is relevant *per se*.

Part of the blame for the disappointing positive and normative outcomes generated by orthodox theories is due to the recurring analytical focus on the statics and the comparative statics of trade liberalization; while insufficient attention has been devoted to the dynamic issues, undoubtedly much harder to analyze formally and to test with the traditional quantitative tools.

The Static and Dynamic Consequences of Trade Liberalization

It is widely accepted that trade enhances income in a variety of ways. It allows specialization, so that domestic producers can concentrate in those industries where their efficiency is higher, relative to foreign producers. Therefore, exports make it possible to buy from abroad commodities which would be relatively expensive to produce at home. Welfare then increases both because specialization raises the purchasing power of the country on the international markets; and because consumers can buy a wider variety of goods at cheaper prices, from foreign producers (imports) and often also from more efficient influence policies, so that the existing distortions are not removed, or that new "desirable" measures are introduced. The value of the resources devoted to these rent-seeking (or rent-keeping) activities is a deadweight loss for the economy, which rises with the fragility of governments and with the consequences of trade liberalization for the inefficient firms.

Thanks to academic research and empirical evidence, it is now apparent that the dynamic and rent-seeking effects are more promising avenues of investigation. Both imply that much more weight should therefore be devoted to the institutional aspects of economic development and growth. The positive and normative results generated by the classical and neo-classical views cannot be disregarded altogether, but a shift in focus is in order.

ON THE ROLE OF TRADE IN RICH AND POOR COUNTRIES

One way to consider how protectionism affects welfare and growth from an institutional viewpoint is by observing that the nature of the positive and normative link between trade, income levels and growth rates in a high-income country differs from that in a typical UDC.

Developed countries feature low information and transaction costs. Trade barriers are not absent, but they must usually be justified to the public opinion and accepted by a large enough groups of coalitions. Failure to meet these requirements often implies a loss of consensus, resources and legitimacy for the incumbent politicians. Surely, these guidelines do not make sure that free trade prevails; in fact it doesn't. But they are strict enough to bring about a considerable reduction in the possibility of using trade policies for rent-seeking purposes.

On the other hand, UDCs are typically ruled by rent-seeking autocrats, whose power is not legitimized by popular consensus. In these countries the ruling *élites* engage in systematic rent-seeking by means of discretionary policies, sometimes enforced by means of violence. Thus, policies serve the double purpose of extracting rents, and of securing ongoing support from the relevant coalitions. Trade policies are no exception. Trade liberalization as such may of course be a policy; but it would be fallacious to believe that in the absence of an exogenous shock free trade leads to--or stands for--a truly free-market, growth-enhancing attitude[1]

The Rich Country Case

A rich country can be defined as one where productivity is relatively high. An indicator may be the relative size of the service sector (nontradables), which in these economies usually absorbs the majority of resources devoted to production. This means that most of the opportunities offered by specialization and technical progress have already been taken advantage of. Producers face the correct set of incentives, which lead them to behave efficiently. In this light, the introduction of a modest degree of protectionism[2]--say, to satisfy workers in an industry affected by a negative shock--does not reduce income significantly. Technologies cannot be destroyed; the effects on the economies of scales are likely to be moderate; and the expected returns on rent-seeking activities may be stifled by a high degree of product substitutability, foreign direct investments, uncertainty about the time span during which the rent extraction can be carried out.

In short, protectionism may indeed affect future income growth; but it is plausible to contend that in the short-to-medium run, protectionism is "just" a matter of income redistribution. The protected industries have a benefit, which is paid by the rest of the economy (including consumers, of course). The resulting deadweight loss for society mainly coincides with the rent-seeking efforts of the would-be beneficiaries of the proposed trade policies. Other kinds of inefficiencies are hardly relevant before the dynamic effects come to the surface and are clearly perceived. Indeed, after a change in the terms of trade has occurred, trade policies may actually reduce the need to shift resources from one industry to another in order to respond to the new structure of comparative advantages. And in a

---

[1] A Detailed analysis of the autocrat's behavior from a public-choice and institutional point of view is presented in E. Colombatto and J. Macey, "Information and Transaction costs as the Determinants of Politically Tolerable Growth Levels," *Working Paper Series*, International Centre for Economic Research, (No 11, 1997).

[2] A modest degree of protectionism is one which does not justify significant rent-seeking activities by producers, who therefore do not engage in law-bargaining with politicians.

short-run perspective the benefits from lower adjustment costs may even overcompensate for distortions.

This is consistent with the recent history of trade policy, and explains why "temporary" and "targeted" trade restrictions are so popular in the OECD area, and also easily tolerated within the WTO/GATT framework. They are allegedly introduced in order to distribute adjustment costs over a relatively long period of time, so as to reduce losses of income; and they are targeted, so as to signal a commitment to help injured industries only, rather than a generalized drive towards protectionism.

The link between trade and growth in relatively rich economies has become rather complicated for a variety of reasons. It is relatively easy to pass protectionist bills or to enforce protectionism *de facto*, especially if targeted at weak industries. As argued earlier, such a policy is accepted since it is perceived as a government commitment to provide insurance against negative sectoral shocks. The need for such a commitment is higher, the lower the growth rate in other parts of the world; and the higher domestic unemployment, which keeps the demand for social insurance high. However, trade policies may be harder and harder to tolerate in the long run, due to the increasing costs in terms of missed growth opportunities.

Within this framework the problem for the policy maker is to strike a satisfactory balance between the use of trade policy, which provides social insurance, preserves the existing income distribution pattern, has limited cost in the short run; and the long-run negative consequences it has on growth, which make trade policy unsustainable. In the past couple of decades the solution to this problem has been solved by applying the so-called fair-trade principle, whereby non-tariff barriers are *de facto* enforced by the Executive on a totally discretionary basis. In particular, discretion refers to the length of time during which the measures are taken, as well as to the set of commodities and to the range of exporting countries involved. By means of fair trade, politicians have the flexibility they need to provide social insurance, but also to phase it out when its cost for the economy as a whole becomes exceedingly high. In particular, by shifting responsibility to the Executive, the policy makers can elude the pressure of coalitions at parliamentary or congressional level (the legislative body usually maintains responsibility for the welfare state, though), and they can also generate some kind of "rotating protection", whereby the overall rate of protection may remain constant, but the beneficiaries change and one coalition can be played against the other.[1]

The Poor Country Case,

The above is in contrast with the UDC case, where productivity is low, and most resources are devoted to the production of tradable goods, mainly manufactured and agricultural. Under these circumstances free trade as such may be important, but not crucial. Inefficiencies are so diffused that there are plenty of other possibilities of improving economic performance. In fact, the most important origin of economic backwardness is the lack of the rule of law. That is, the institutional framework is ill-defined and/or unreliable, so that investment is discouraged, both in fixed and in human capital. The presence of free trade alone is not enough to restore confidence. Actually, the presence of some protectionism would hardly be a problem, if the rules of game were clear enough, and the rent-seeking activities of the ruling *élite* predictable. Indeed, it would not be impossible to argue that under some circumstances moderate trade restrictions may help in making the economic and political framework more stable.

It is undeniable, however, that trade liberalization represents an important signal to the business community. A commitment to free trade means that the ruling *élite* is willing to relinquish an easy, politically acceptable avenue for rent-seeking, possibly for the sake of sustained growth. By giving up protectionism politicians demonstrate that they are taking steps away from the roving-bandit attitude, and that future policies will be aimed at acquiring consensus and legitimacy by means of economic results, rather than through violence. In addition, the departure from protectionism makes all other policies more transparent and therefore reduces discretion and law-bargaining.

For instance, free trade transforms the exchange rate into a quality indicator as regards monetary policy. Discretionary help to badly managed companies becomes much more visible, and thus less viable. Similarly, attempts by the authorities to sidestep the constraints imposed by a free-trade regime are an equally powerful indicator about

---

[1] See D. Verdier, *Democracy and International Trade*, (Princeton: Princeton University Press, 1994).

the real attitude of the political decision maker--the cost of sidestepping thus becomes larger in terms of credibility.

From this viewpoint, it can be shown that the orthodox debate on the role of trade policies for growth in UDCs has not been about the role of trade, but rather about the dynamics of income distribution and the role of government intervention; not only on trade matters, of course. This is of some consequence, for it helps clear the ground from a number of common misconceptions. The most important of them perhaps regards the controversy on import substitution and export promotion in UDCs.

Contrary to conventional beliefs, the positive effect of trade *per se* on growth was never questioned, not even by the supporters of the original (ECLA) import-substitution approach. In fact these always took care to emphasize the need for regional coordination--a synonym for free-trade areas--in order to encourage specialization, allow economies of scale in production, and competition within the various industries. Import substitution did not imply protectionism based on some kind of infant-industry argument, either. In fact, import-substitution neglected the possibility of experiencing learning-by-doing processes. Rather, the core of the argument was focused on the concept that the comparative-advantage structures of the "centre" and of the "periphery" could not change spontaneously, but only by means of government intervention. It was widely believed that without government intervention, UDCs would have been stuck in industries where productivity growth was slow, whereas the developed countries would have taken advantage of the faster technological change typical of manufactures. In other words, in the light of import substitution, government intervention and trade policies were not aimed at restricting trade *per se*; instead, they were supposed to force an economy to change its comparative-advantage.

The crucial issue was not the idea that protectionism is good for growth, but rather that government intervention is necessary in order to change the country's comparative advantage, so as to create more favorable trade opportunities in the future. Clearly, entrepreneurs--both domestic and foreign--were supposed to be unable to change their investment strategies autonomously, following the dynamics of sectoral productivity, and had to be encouraged to do so by government intervention. In theory, this is not without some logic. If producers face the wrong incentive structure; that is if agents benefit from substantial rent-seeking in the industries where comparative advantage is fading away, government intervention will be required in order to persuade them that at least comparable amounts of rents are guaranteed in the "winning" industries as well. From this standpoint, import-substitution strategies would have been acceptable, even if as a third-best solution to the wrong pattern of specialization provoked by rent-seeking. Clearly, the first-best solution would have been the elimination of rent-seeking altogether; while free trade with subsidies financed by lump-sum taxes would be second-best.

THE ROLE OF INSTITUTIONS RECONSIDERED

The argument developed in the previous paragraphs shows that the link between trade and growth is complex. In developed countries the trade regime probably will not affect growth in the short run. On the contrary, in most OECD countries the public considers the government trade-policy attitude to be a tell-tale sign of its commitment to social-insurance programs. The importance of such a commitment is greater, as the possibility of suffering from exogenous negative shocks and the amount of unemployed resources increase. But in order to retain consensus, refusal to use the trade-policy signal in order to improve long-run growth prospects must be replaced by other signals.

Obvious policy substitutes for protectionism are industrial policies to satisfy specific pressure groups and the welfare state to appease diffused interests. This is consistent with economic history in the OECD bloc of countries after World War II: overall protectionism has declined, but industrial policies have been playing a major role in many countries, and the welfare state expanded considerably.

Other priorities usually prevail in undeveloped economies. On the one hand, the public demands higher growth so as to attain improved living standards. On the other hand, the ruling *élite* aims at preserving its rent-seeking opportunities and, more generally, power. From this viewpoint, the trade regime is often a secondary element and it generally suits the interest of the incumbent politicians, more than the needs of the population. This holds also if the incumbent rulers are forced to enhance growth in order to preserve power;[1] then a

---

[1] This has been a convincing explanation of several success stories, especially in Southeast Asia. See on this S. Haggard, *Pathways from the Periphery* (Ithaca:

moderate amount of protectionism can still be tolerated. However, in small countries free trade soon becomes necessary to sustain growth, whereas in very large countries moderate protectionism can be sustained for much longer periods, provided the domestic market is characterized by competitive behavior.

In this light, free-trade in UDCs is also a signal. But in order to be meaningful, trade liberalization must accompany and confer credibility to other policy acts aiming towards a free-market institutional context. Capital movement and increased dependence on foreign capital would indeed be a primary example, for capital movement liberalization would lose much of its effectiveness if the policy makers retained the right to interfere with trade flows.

Institutions and Growth

The critical result of the argument developed so far is that the questions on trade and growth raised in the traditional literature are correct and important. But the conceptual tools which have been used to answer them have been inappropriate. In particular, the orthodox tradition deals with growth by focusing on the variables which affect income; but neglects to study the variables that affect growth. Much work has been done on how to take advantage of the existing technology, on the optimal way to use the available resources by solving market and/or government failures through more or less "ideal" policies, whereby agents react to the policies, rather than to the perceived opportunities to engage in profitable law-bargaining games by advocating additional intervention. In fact, the opposite is more likely to be true.

The orthodox approach is perhaps an acceptable standpoint when examining developed countries in a short- to medium-run perspective. Distorted incentives and rent-seeking opportunities usually take time to register negative effects on growth. The short-run costs reflect relatively small static inefficiencies. This helps understand why it is fairly easy to pass policies aimed at tampering with market forces for the sake of what the median voter appreciates as "more desirable" income distributions--or more desirable ways to preserve or

---

Cornell University Press, 1990); and also J. E. Campos and H. Root, *The Key to the Asian Miracle* (Washington D.C.: Brookings Institution, 1996).

remodel income distribution after some exogenous change has taken place.

Nevertheless, it should be clear that growth does not depend on trade policy, but on the institutional arrangements that create a suitable system of incentives, reward innovation, allow performing firms to come to the surface at the expense of inefficient competitors, and make it easy for resources to be shifted from one industry to another. A free trade regime *per se* is of course important, but only as long as it is part of a credible and "neutral" institutional framework, where government intervention is not zero, but interferes very little with the individual decision-making process. Otherwise the trade regime--whatever the amount of openness it is associated with--conveys ambiguous signals, and thus plays a very minor role.

This applies to both developed and developing countries, with an important difference. In the former case growth is slowed down by the political need to gather enough consensus. In turn, consensus is acquired through income distribution and redistribution policies. The role of trade therefore depends on how trade policies can be employed to this purpose. In the latter case (UDCs) growth depends on the quality and stability of the institutional framework; on the rule of law. Free trade is not essential; some protectionism may even be necessary, especially if it makes political behavior more stable and credible. Surely, free trade matters for the sustainability of long-run growth, but unfortunately that is hardly an issue for most undeveloped countries because such countries are focused exclusively on the short run.

Institutions and Trade

One might conclude that trade policies will seldom be used in developed countries, where the rule of law is taken for granted. Protectionism gives short-term benefits, but it also entails short-term costs (retaliation from abroad), and is politically costly to repeal when it becomes too harmful to growth. Other tools are preferable. Thus trade barriers are relatively low in rich countries. But the causal link between free trade and high income is indirect. Policy makers do not keep trade barriers low because they want to maximize growth. They keep them low, because protectionism is not the best way to create sustainable rent-seeking opportunities in high-technology, low transaction cost economies.

Where growth is below expectations due to pervasive distortions, and public opinion's demand for institutional change is high, free trade is necessary in order to get the relative price structure right and--perhaps more important from the policy makers' viewpoint--to improve the welfare of the median voter. In other words, trade policy becomes a liability when growth becomes a political priority, as protectionism serves those who benefit from arrangements detrimental to growth. Free trade is then a valuable tool to bring about institutional change by mobilizing public opinion in favor of growth. If institutional change turns out to be successful, then growth follows. But the correlation between free trade and high growth remains spurious, for better economic performance follows from institutional improvements (including free trade), not from free trade as such.

By contrast, in poor countries trade policies are used by the autocrat in order to create and extract rents. In these countries, government intervention does not necessarily mean low trade volumes. Indeed the opposite may be true. Autocrats are aware that the ruling coalition can extract rents as long as its citizens cannot hide their income and their wealth. Controlling wealth is relatively easy if capital movements and convertibility can be restricted; and smuggling remains limited. But in many countries where monitoring of wealth flows is expensive and local-community ties relatively strong, de-specialization in production, barter and self-consumption move much of the economy underground[1]. In these situations the autocrat will try to increase foreign trade in order to extract rents by taxing or licensing import/export flows when they get across the border, as long as (a) the border is not too porous, and (b) trade is managed by a limited number of "friendly agents"; otherwise new interest groups could come to the surface and become a threat for the incumbent *élites*.

Surely, the traditional controversy between import substitution and export promotion is of less importance, if not irrelevant, since the desirability of openness *per se* was never questioned by serious scholars. In fact, the original import-substitution thesis was not against

---

[1] It may be worth pointing out that this actually took place on a huge scale in Russia during the Civil War (1918-21), as peasants reacted to administered prices on agricultural products imposed by the Bolsheviks. Sales of such products to the cities and to the Red Army collapsed; and so did purchases of manufactured products from the cities. The rural communities then devoted more and more resources to the local production of tools, textiles, etc.. See O. Figes, *A People's Tragedy* (London: Jonathan Cape, 1996), ch. 13.

trade, but rather it took for granted that economic agents would not react to market signals. And that is possible only if agents enjoy significant rents, the size and depth of which depend of course on the institutional framework. The "opening up" of UDCs will be virtually worthless unless the institutional distortions caused by rent-seeking in these countries are removed.

SUGGESTED READINGS

H. W. Arndt, *Economic Development, the History of an Idea*, (Chicago: University of Chicago Press, 1987).

J. Bhagwati, *Protectionism*, (Cambridge: MIT Press, 1988).

D. Lal, *The Poverty of 'Development Economics'*, (Cambridge: Harvard University Press, 1985).

PART FOUR

PROPERTY RIGHTS AND BUSINESS FIRMS

Chapter 12

THE FIRM AND CONTRACTS

Suppose I buy a wheat-producing farm. I can organize production on the farm in two ways. I could enter into a contractual agreement with one person to grow wheat on my land, with another to harvest it, with a third to store it, and with a fourth to sell it. I negotiate a separate agreement with contractual partners and pay each of them an agreed upon sum of money (or whatever else the contract says) in exchange for a specific performance. This method of organizing production is called *contracting across markets.*

Alternatively, I might contract with the same four people to work for me as a team. I pay each person a specific sum of money in exchange for the right to tell each of them what to do, when to do it, and how to do it. In this case, I am the central contractual agent in a team production process. This method of organizing production is called the firm. *The firm is a group of people in teamwork.*

The costs of contracting across markets include identifying the lowest-cost partners, negotiating contracts, renegotiating contracts in response to changing circumstances,[1] and reducing the probability of opportunistic behavior. An advantage of contracting across markets is that the cost of shirking is borne by the shirker, who is paid the same amount of money (less possible damages) whether fulfilling that side of the bargain in five hours or five days.

The team method of production is costly, too. A member of the team must have incentives to incur the cost of monitoring the performance of the team. The team method of production requires specialists to supervise the division of tasks up and down the chain of production. Finally, there is no way of telling who contributed how much to the total output of the firm creating a problem of relating the rewards and productivity of cooperating inputs.

---

[1] Reopening of the Suez Canal after the 1956 war between Egypt and Israel led to numerous renegotiations (and suits) of contracts to build oil tankers, most of them having to do with the size of tankers.

Transaction costs, the complexities of large operations, and limitations on the supply of managerial skills eventually increase the cost of the team method of production relative to the cost of contracting across markets. Those firms that are successful in discovering a less costly mix of internal and external transactions do better than others.

The firm in neoclassical economics is a black box that has the objective of profit maximization. Given the state of the art, the equilibrium solution shows what the price-output decision of the firm would have been if we had perfect foresight, if the internal relations within the firm didn't matter, and if no new knowledge interfered with the model. In treating the firm as a black box, the theory suffers several important limitations. First, it describes only the outcome arising in a regime of private property rights and insignificant transaction costs. Next, the neoclassical view of the firm assumes either that all members of the team have the same objective or that the objective of profit maximization could be enforced at zero (or the same) costs regardless of the nature of internal agreements between members of the team and regardless of differences in property rights. Finally, it views gains in productivity as arising from specialization among independent producers across markets rather than from successful internal contracting among the team members.

In a world of different property rights, which is the subject of this book, the neoclassical model of the firm has little explanatory value.

THE FIRM

We observe teamwork because it is an efficient method for organizing production. Business firms exists because they are organizations that make teamwork efficient. *The firm is a nexus of a set of contracts among individuals involving the use of resources they own or control.* The survival requirement of the team is that the value of its output must exceed the sum of the market values each member of the team could produce contracting across markets. Some twenty years ago Armen Alchian wrote:

> The wealth growth of General Electric derives precisely from the superiority of its internal markets for exchange and

reallocation of resources--a superiority arising from the greater (cheaper) information about people and proposals. Many knowledge effects that would be externalistic in an ordinary market are converted into beneficial internalities within the firm as incentives and rewards to those producing them.[1]

A major threat to the survival of the firm arises from the fact that members of the team have their own private ends. The performance of the team depends on cooperation and coordination among its members. And cooperation and coordination among team members depend on contractual agreements they have with one another.

The efficiency of the firm then arises from the set of contracts, which are the agreements about (1) future performance of members of the team, and (2) metering performance and rewards. Agreements on metering productivity and rewards are critical because the firm's output is produced by many cooperating inputs, and there is no way to tell who has contributed how much to the total product.

Successful contracts enhance coordination and cooperation among team members. And the commitment to work together reduces transaction costs. In a world of uncertainty and incomplete information, different kinds of contracts (constrained by prevailing property rights) create their own incentives and transaction costs. Those incentives and transaction costs then, through their effect on rewards, encourage productivity responses. That is, property rights, contractual agreements, and transaction costs determine the marginal productivity of inputs used by the firm. Jensen and Meckling wrote:

> Statutory laws set bounds on the kinds of contracts into which individuals and organizations may enter without risking criminal prosecution.... The courts adjudicate conflicts between contracting parties and establish precedents which form the body of common law. All of these government activities affect both the kinds of contracts and the extent to which contracting

---

[1] A. Alchian, "Corporate Management and Property Rights," in *The Economics of Property Rights*, E. Furubotn and S. Pejovich, eds. (Cambridge: Ballinger, 1974), p. 142.

is relied upon. This in turn determines the usefulness, productivity, profitability and viability of [business firms].[1]

Some types of contracts pass the market test and are imitated. While the terms of those contracts might differ in specific details from one firm to another, they attach specific names to different types of firms, such as corporations, partnerships, cooperatives, labor-managed firms, etc.

CONTRACTS AND REWARDS

In a very interesting example, Armen Alchian and William Allen discuss the effects of property rights and contracts on the performance of teamwork.[2]

There is an island called Fishland. On this island 1,000 people fish for a living. They fish from the shore and each of them averages four fish per day. The total daily catch is thus 4,000 fish. Then a boat is found. The boat makes it possible for some to fish on the ocean. At issue is the effect of new technology or the new production function on the community's wealth.

Table 12-1 provides hypothetical data on the quantities of fish that can be caught by varying the number of people on the boat.[3] The example specifies the effects of property rights in the boat and contractual agreements among the team members on the total output, rewards, location of risk, and incentives.

Share and Share Alike

Suppose that those already on the boat share the daily catch and jointly control how many additional persons are to fish from the boat. This type of property right, which is similar to communal property as

---

[1] M. Jensen, and W. Meckling, "Theory of the Firm: Managerial Behavior, Agency Costs and Ownership Structure," *Journal of Financial Economics* 3 (1976), p. 311.

[2] Discussion in this section is adapted from A. Alchian and W. Allen, *Exchange and Production*, (Belmont: Wadsworth Publishing Co. 1983), chapter 8.

[3] Net social marginal product in column five is the marginal product on board less the opportunity costs of four fish from the shore.

discussed in chapter five, provides people on the boat with the flow of benefits from the daily catch only for as long as they are members of the team.

Team members have incentives to use the effect of an additional person on their own average daily catch as the criterion for determining whether that person should be allowed on board. In our case, the number of people on the boat is likely to be three. The total output is 4,012 fish. The gain is captured by people allowed to fish from the boat. Labor-managed firms, producers' cooperatives, and some professional associations such as those of doctors, lawyers, musicians and electricians are examples of this type of teamwork.

If and when such payments were legal and not too costly to collect, those already on board would have incentives to invite additional people to fish from the boat at the price of a daily entry fee. Clearly, the fee must assure the newcomer of a little more than four fish per day, and, at the same time, must make those on board a little better off. In our example, taking a fourth person on the boat would reduce the average daily catch from 8 to 7.5 fish. However, the fourth person could pay a fee of 3 fish per day and keep 4.5 fish for himself. Those already on board should be happy to accept a fee-paying newcomer because they would end up with 8.5 fish per day. This type of arrangement is found in many country clubs and some labor unions.

Each member of the team has incentives to shirk and stop others from shirking. A shirking worker captures all the benefits of that action and shifts the costs of reduced output to the team. For example, one person sleeps for a few hours (without co-workers noticing this absence) and the total catch of fish is reduced from 24 to 21. They all get seven fish. The shirker has traded one fish for several hours of leisure. That is a voluntary choice, and we have to assume that the shirker is better off. The other two people lost one fish each. Monitoring each other in a small group could create animosities and disrupt cooperation of members of the team. A larger group needs a professional monitor. In either case the cost of monitoring team is high. The following story suggests two sources of transaction costs in the type of arrangement discussed here. First, there is the cost of either self-policing or hiring a professional to enforce no-shirking behavior. Second, since the team hires the monitor, the latter has incentives to relax no-shirking rule.

On the Yangtze River in China, there is a section of fast water over which boats are pulled upstream by a team of coolies prodded by an overseer using a whip. On one such passage an American lady, horrified by the sight of the overseer whipping the men as they strained at their harness, demanded that something be done about the brutality. She was quickly informed by the captain that nothing could be done: "Those men own the right to draw boats over this stretch of water and they have hired the overseer and given him his duties."[1]

Table 12-1. Fishland

Number of Men on Board	Total Catch on Board	MP on Board	Average Product on Board	Net Social MP	Social Total
0	0	0	0	0	4,000
1	6	6	6	2	4,002
2	16	10	8	6	4,008
3	24	8	8	4	4,0012
4	30	6	7.5	2	4,0014
5	34	4	6.8	0	4,0014
6	36	2	6	-2	4,0012
7	36	0	5.14	-4	4,008
8	32	-4	4	-8	4,000
9	27	-5	3	-9	3,991
10	21	-6	2.1	-10	3,981

Source: A. Alchian and W. Allen, *Exchange and Production*, p. 164.

The risk of fluctuations in the daily catch (bad luck, fish not biting, bad weather, problems with the boat, etc.) is borne by members of the team. Should a member want to avoid this risk, the only way out is to quit the boat. The cost of leaving the boat is the difference between the average daily catch from fishing on the ocean and the expected daily catch from the shore.

Incentives to innovate, invest in new equipment, and maintain the boat depend on the time horizon of members of the team. The

---

[1] J. McManus, "The Cost of Alternative Economic Organizations," *Canadian Journal of Economics* 8 (1975), p. 335.

shorter is the period of time they expect to fish on the boat, the less incentives they would have to sacrifice their current income for future benefits they are not going to be around to capture.

The Discoverer of the Boat Has the Right of Ownership

Suppose the man who found the boat becomes its owner. He hires people, pays them wages to fish for him, and keeps everything (i.e., the residual) that is left after all contractual obligations are met. To hire someone, the owner must pay that person just a little over four fish per day. The owner has incentives to hire five people. The marginal product of hiring the fifth equals that person's opportunity costs. The total output of 1,014 fish is equal to the social maximum. As Alchian and Allen note:

> The coincidence between maximum private and maximum social gain is not accidental. People with private property rights who seek profits in an open market system will maximize the social total.... It is not a contrived quirk of our special example, and it happens without the profit seeker's intent or a central directive authority.[1]

The owner has incentives to incur the costs of monitoring members of the team. Unlike in our previous case, the monitor, who now works for the owner, has no incentives to overlook some shirking.
    The owner has incentives to innovate, invest in new equipment, and maintain the boat because he bears the costs of maintenance, and captures the future benefits that his current sacrifices make possible, regardless of the length of time he plans to keep the boat. That is so because the owner can avoid the risk of fluctuations in the catch (i.e., changes in his wealth) by selling the boat and capturing the value of expected future gains in one lump sum.

---

[1] A. Alchian, and W. Allen, *Exchange and Production*, p. 167.

Contracts to Rent

Instead of hiring people to work for him, the owner might rent the boat to a person or a group of people. The question is then how many people are likely to end up on the boat, and what is the maximum rent the owner can extract from them? If the owner rented his boat to three people, their total catch would be 24 fish, or 12 fish over and above their opportunity costs. The maximum rent the owner can get with three people renting the boat is thus a bit below 12 fish. If the owner rented the boat to five persons, their total catch would be 34 fish, or 14 fish over and above their opportunity costs. Given the data in our example, the maximum rent the owner can get is then just about 14 fish. The outcome seems to be the same as in the previous example (hiring people at a wage of 4+ fish).

What then is the difference, if any, between the owner hiring five people and his renting the boat to five people? Assuming perfect foresight about the daily catch, there is no difference. But in a world of uncertainty and imperfect knowledge, the two arrangements are not the same in terms of incentives and risk. Under the hiring arrangement, the owner bears the costs (and gets the benefits) from unforeseen fluctuations in the daily catch. Under the leasing arrangement, the renters bear those costs in the short run. Also, they have no incentives to maintain the boat properly. Michael Jensen and William Meckling wrote:

> The obvious agency costs of the rental arrangement are those associated with the reduced incentives for the user to maintain the asset properly, to guard it from theft, and the increased incentives to misuse it...The magnitude of these costs along with monitoring and bonding costs that would be incurred in the effort to control them explains why rental of most durable goods is not observed. It is simply a more costly contracting arrangement.[1]

---

[1] M. Jensen, and W. Meckling, "Rights and Production Functions," *Journal of Business* 52 (1979), p. 480. J&M define agency costs as the sum of the monitoring expenditures by the principal, the bonding expenditures by the agent, and the residual loss.

Everyone Can Fish From The Boat

Suppose the government decides that the boat is communal property (belongs to all people). In that case, everyone who wants to fish from the boat can do so. How many people would end up on the boat? As long as the average product on board exceeds four fish, people will have incentives to continue joining the crew. Eventually, there will be eight people on the boat, each of them catching just about as many fish as they could catch from the shore. The community ends up with 4,000 fish. No member of the community is better off. And no one has incentives to maintain the boat.

Government Decides Who Can Fish from the Boat

Suppose the government appoints a manager who is told to maximize income from the right to fish on the ocean. The profit of 14 fish goes to the state. It would appear that the only difference between private and state ownership is who gets the profit. However, that is not true. The maximum profit is not known in advance. The issues are: What are decision makers' incentives to discover and seek larger profits, and what are the transaction costs of monitoring their behavior?

No one in the government can appropriate the residual, incentives to invest time and effort to seek the best profits are certainly not very strong, and no one bears the entire risk of making inefficient decisions. The loss is shared by taxpayers. The actual outcome thus depends on the private ends of those who manage government-owned resources, the private ends of their superiors, and the superiors' transaction costs of monitoring managers. This is not to say that decision makers in government will never try to maximize profit. But compared to the private owner, they simply have weaker incentives to do so.

Usefulness of the Fishland Example[1]

The Fishland example allows us to understand the effects of different property rights on incentives affecting human behavior. It shows that

---

[1] This section is based on comments I received from Laszlo Szakadat, a young economist from the University of Budapest.

the regime of private property rights, compared to other types of arrangements discussed in the example, creates more incentives for individuals to bear the costs of owning more boats because they capture all the future benefits. And because of that, the cost of making new boats (in terms of fish forgone) would control the rate at which new boats are produced. In the process, market competition would transfer income from the owners of boats to those who own the resources required to make boats (*via* higher prices for those resources) and to consumers (through a lower price for fish). Finally, the market competition continuously creates new knowledge (better fishing areas), stimulates innovations (better technology), and encourages imitations of successful activities.

TEAMWORK AND TRANSACTION COSTS

Two major sources of transaction costs in business firms are *bounded rationality* and *opportunism*. In one way or another, bounded rationality has been discussed throughout this book. It simply means that in a world of uncertainty and incomplete knowledge, individuals have different subjective perceptions of the real world and limited ability to predict the future. As noted in the Fishland example, an important implication of bounded rationality is the consequences of the allocation of risk under different property rights on the outcome of human interactions.

A major difference between private property rights and all other types of property rights lies in the distribution of risk. The owner can sell a risky asset and invest proceeds in private savings. Or a person can take money from the bank and invest in a risky venture. An individual can keep an oil well, hoping that its reserves are large, or sell it and invest proceeds in less risky assets. I can be paid my opportunity cost and bear the risk of changes in the demand for my skill. Or I can shift that risk to my employer (at a price) through a long-term employment contract.

On the other hand, the nontransferability of assets provides no room for specialization of risk bearing across individuals with different degrees of risk aversion. In a socialist economy I can neither choose risk nor avoid bearing it. One can vote with one's feet, but that is a costly alternative. In a socialist economy, those who bear risk (i.e., ordinary people who are affected by decisions) and those who are in a position to economize on transaction costs (i.e., individuals who make decisions) are not the same people. That is, incentives to resolve contractually the conflicting objectives of individuals with respect to the risk of a decision are much weaker and not always possible. In a capitalist economy those incentives are strong. Implications for differences in transaction costs under different property rights arrangements are obvious.

Opportunism follows from bounded rationality and self-interest. Armen Alchian and Susan Woodward defined opportunism and its implications for transaction costs as follows:

> When a conflict arises between what people want and what they have agreed to do for others, they will act in their own interest insofar as it is costly for others to know their behavior....Opportunism covers more than the propensity for mutually reliant parties to mislead, distort, disguise, obfuscate, or otherwise confuse in order to expropriate wealth from one another. It includes honest disagreements. Even when both parties recognize the genuine goodwill of the other, different but honest perceptions can lead to disputes that are costly to resolve.[1]

The so-called Lange-Mises controversy is a good example of failure to recognize the importance of transaction costs arising from opportunism. The proposition that ignited the debate was that the planned economy could duplicate the results of the private property economy if the managers of socialist firms were instructed to maximize profits. Neoclassical economics provided the framework for the debate. Given the assumption of insignificant transaction costs, socialist managers had to follow instructions from the ruling elite. Hence the debate focused on the comparison of equilibrium solutions. The result was an impeccable technical discussion that wasted lots of resources on the wrong issue.

The issue of the debate should have been whether managers of socialist firms are going to follow instructions; if so, why so; and if not, why not? Recognizing that positive transaction costs encourage opportunistic behavior, relevant questions for analysis should have

---

[1] A. Alchian, and S. Woodward, "The Firm is Dead; Long Live the Firm," *Journal of Economic Literature* 26 (1988), p. 66.

been: What is the socialist manager's survival trait? What is the penalty-reward system under which that manager operates? What is the cost of monitoring the manager's behavior? What would the manager gain from pursuing planned objectives? Could the manager do better by pursuing another kind of activity within the constraints of transaction costs? The next two chapters address these and similar questions.

Opportunism has two basic forms: *hold-up* and *moral hazard*. Both create incentives to prevent opportunistic behavior *via* reductions in transaction costs. However, those incentives have different consequences. Hold-up explains incentives for vertical integration, while moral hazard explains the principal-agent conflict.

To understand the implications of hold-up it is necessary to distinguish between specific and general resources. Resources are general if the wealth of their owners does not depend on the behavior of any specific member of the team (e.g., tenants in the building paying market price for office space, or the owner of furniture used in the building's lobby).

On the other hand, a resource is specific to the firm if the wealth of the owner of that resource is affected by the behavior of other members of the team. Usually, large sunk costs create opportunities for hold-up. For example, I own the only elevator in a building. The building is specific to my elevator. I can affect the building owner's wealth by restricting the use of elevator to certain hours or claiming frequent repairs. The building owner would then either have to reduce monthly rental or lose tenants.

By holding the building owner up, I could appropriate (by raising rental for the elevator) the difference between daily revenues from the building and daily operating costs plus the daily equivalent of the building's salvage value; or the difference between daily revenues from the building and the daily equivalent of the cost of another elevator.[1] Frequently, resources are specific to each other (e.g., oil well, pipeline and refinery).

Those who own resources specific to the firm have incentives to bear the costs of protecting themselves from opportunistic behavior by other members of the team. The two best known methods of protection against hold-up are vertical integration and long-term

---

[1] For analysis including numerous examples see B. Klein, R. Crawford, and A. Alchian, "Vertical Integration, Appropriable Rents, and the Competitive Contracting Process," *Journal of law and Economics* 21 (1978).

contracts. Vertical integration rules out opportunistic behavior but might run into problems with government agencies such as the Federal Trade Commission, Federal Communications Commission, and the Antitrust Division of the Department of Justice. Long-term contracts do not eliminate opportunistic behavior, but bypassing legal problems with the government might be efficient when the appropriable rent is low or contracts are relatively inexpensive to specify and monitor (goodwill, brand names, rental of land). At any rate, protecting firm-specific assets from opportunistic behavior reduces transaction costs. And lower transaction costs translate into higher productivity for the firm.

Moral hazard (or postcontractual opportunism) occurs when one party to a contract relies on the behavior of another party and information about that behavior is costly. The source of moral hazard is agency costs and plasticity of resources. Jensen and Meckling explained agency costs as follows:

> If both parties to the relationship are utility maximizers there is good reason to believe that the agent will not always act in the best interests of the principal.... It is generally impossible for the principal or the agent at zero cost to ensure that the agent will make optimal decisions from the principal's viewpoint. In most agency relationships the principal and the agent will incur positive monitoring costs.... We define agency costs as the sum of: (1) the monitoring expenditures by the principal, (2) the bonding expenditures by the agent, (3) the residual loss.[1]

Resources are plastic when the agent has a wide range of legitimate discretionary choices and the principal faces high transaction costs of ensuring that a particular agenda is pursued. For example, teachers have a great deal of freedom from their academic superiors to teach what they like. Researchers in drug companies could easily spend their time experimenting with new drugs rather than improving known and profitable ones. And imagine the shareholders and/or debt holders controlling the work of fashion designers. In contrast, railroads, steel-producing firms, pizza establishments, and utilities are not plastic.

Because of high costs of preventing opportunistic behavior (not because of higher risk), firms with plastic assets should be

---

[1] M. Jensen, and W. Meckling, Theory of the Firm," p.308.

expected to find borrowing more costly. A testable implication is that firms with plastic assets have relatively lower debt-equity ratios. Alchian and Woodward made the following point:

> By "plastic" we do not simply mean risky. Oil that has only to be pumped and sold is highly implastic. The optimal rate at which to pump the oil depends on the pattern of prices over time, and there is little in the way of possibilities for exploiting an oil well either by increasing the riskiness of its value or by changing its product into personal consumption. But an oil is a risky asset.[1]

Economic analysis of the firm must then: (1) recognize that the subjective perceptions individuals form about their opportunity sets and trade-offs differ from one person to another, (2) identify property rights in business firms, (3) determine the resultant incentive structures and their effects on the kinds of contractual agreements that emerge through innovations and imitations, (4) deduce the implied behavior of the firm, and (5) examine the propositions yielded by analysis against empirical observations.

SUGGESTED READING

A. Alchian, S. Woodward, "The Firm is Dead: Long Live the Firm," *Journal of Economic Literature* 26 (1988)

M. Jensen, and W. Meckling, "Theory of the Firm: Managerial Behavior, Agency Costs and Ownership Structure," *Journal of Financial Economics* 3 (1976).

---

[1] A. Alchian, and S. Woodward, "The Firm is Dead; Long Live the Firm," p.69.

Chapter 13

CAPITALIST FIRMS

What does it mean when we say that a firm is privately owned? For example, suppose Judy wants to have a Bible shop. She rents a building, borrows money from a local bank to buy equipment, and hires several people to work for her. Laura, on the other hand, wants to run a pornography shop. She owns the building, uses her savings to buy equipment, and members of her family volunteer to help her in the shop. It could appear that Laura owns her business, while Judy has a long way to go to become the owner. In fact, they both own their respective businesses. Why? Because the ownership of the firm is about *rights*. To say that a firm is privately owned means that the owner has a bundle of rights in that firm. Three important rights define the privately owned firm.

The Owner's Right to the Revenue of the Firm

The revenue is used to pay all members of the team their contractual prices. Any residual belongs to the owner. The owner's right to appropriate the residual indicates two specific incentives. One has to do with the choice of assets the owner wants to own; the other is about transaction costs.

The individual who owns firm-specific resources has incentives to pay for the right to control the team--that is, to be the residual taker. Ownership of the firm provides efficient protection against opportunistic behavior by team members who own nonspecific resources. The privately owned firm is then a set of contracts between the owners of cooperating inputs with one party who is common to all the contracts.

The owner's right to appropriate the residual creates incentives for the owner to incur the costs of monitoring team members, to reduce shirking in the firm, to enhance cooperation and coordination of team members, to meter performance and reward employees in accordance with their efforts and productivity, and to change size of the team in response to successful innovations in both technology and managerial techniques.

The Owner's Right to Hire and Fire Members of the Team

The owner must have the right to hire and fire members of the team, or to sue them for damages arising from a breach of contract. Otherwise, the owner's incentives to monitor members of the team would be unenforceable. Employees must also be free to "fire" the employer by quitting, or to sue for damages from a breach of contract. Otherwise, their incentives to seek the highest-valued use for resources they own or control would be ineffective.

In a rule-of-law capitalist economy, the owner has no power to discipline or punish employees, only the right to choose the team. Therein lies the problem with various legal and administrative rules that weaken the owner's right to enter into a contract with a new member of the team and/or to withdraw from a contract with a team member. If in hiring new members of the team the owner had to satisfy criteria not related to the past performance and expected productivity of potential candidates, the team would be smaller, the costs of production would be higher, and marginal firms would not survive. An owner who had to incur high costs in order to justify firing a member of the team would have no credible threat to enforce incentives to supervise and monitor the performance of team members.

The Right to Sell the Preceding Two Rights

The right to transfer one's rights to others at a mutually agreed upon price is a basic component of the right of ownership. The market price of a firm is the value of the bundle of rights. And the value of the bundle of rights is the present value of the expected residual over the firm's life discounted at a rate of interest.

Two critical consequences of the right of ownership on the behavior of the firm are then the owner's right to capitalize the expected future consequences of current decisions about the use of the team into their market prices; and the owner's right to bear changes in the value of the firm. The former eliminates the owner's time horizon because the flow of benefits over the productive life of the firm is available to the owner in one lump sum. The latter creates strong incentives for the owner to seek an ever larger residual.

Compared to neoclassical analysis of the firm, the property rights approach provides a framework for an admittedly less formal but much more predictive analysis of the behavior of a wider class of business enterprises, both within a given set of institutions and under different institutional arrangements. We literally do not know if any firm has ever maximized its profit or operated on its efficiency frontier. Economic analysis cannot answer that question. But it can tell us how and why incentives embedded in private property rights create new knowledge about exchange opportunities and lower the transaction costs of moving resources to their higher-valued uses.

The rest of this chapter examines two different kinds of private-ownership business firms in capitalism: the corporate firm and the codetermining firm. The former emerged voluntarily while the latter was imposed by fiat.

THE CORPORATE FIRM

In a private property, free-market economy, those who own labor, capital and other resources are free to negotiate with each other any kind of teamwork agreement they want. Some types of contracts pass the market test and are repeatedly observed. We economize on identifying those contracts by attaching specific names to firms using those contracts. Thus, we have corporations, single proprietorships, producers' cooperatives, labor cooperatives, associations, not-for-profit firms, partnerships, and other types of teamwork. The contracts of many newspapers, such as the *Wall Street Journal* and *New York Times*, specify objectives that are not consistent with profit maximization. From one firm to another, contracts also differ with respect to informal codes of communication (i.e., internal "cultures").

All those types of firms exist in the United States (and Western Europe). They have all been organized voluntarily and have survived competition from other types of business organizations. No law in the United States dictates the terms of contractual relations among the team members. Yet, the corporate firm has become the dominant type of teamwork. What are the advantages of the corporate firm over other types of private-ownership enterprises?

Technological development around the time of the industrial revolution, improvements in transportation, and the emergence of large political entities in place of feudal princedoms made mass production of goods possible, relatively inexpensive, and profitable. However, mass production of goods required large start-up investment in fixed assets subject to hold-ups. That is, business firms needed a large amount of capital to exploit technological advances and marketing opportunities.

The rule of unlimited liability made the application of new techniques difficult to finance. With each partner held personally liable for the entire debts of the firm, it was too difficult for existing partners to accept new ones. Every partner could impoverish others through incompetence or opportunistic behavior. Moreover, the rule of unlimited liability made absentee ownership costly. In short, the rule restricted equity financing.

In response to economic pressures from within the system, numerous contractual agreements were tried to resolve the problem of pulling together large amounts of capital. Eventually a new legal concept evolved: the rule of limited liability.[1] This law limited each owner's liability to the market value of that individual's investment in the firm. Equity investments were divided into small shares, which were traded in financial markets. The breaking up of equity interests into relatively small shares made it possible for corporate firms to attract funds from small savers.

It follows that the corporate firm has all the advantages of private ownership firms plus more. The corporation has proven to be the most effective method of *voluntarily* gathering large amounts of capital for long-lived ventures. This advantage derives from the anonymous alienability of shares. Anonymity is made possible by limited liability. Individual owners of the firm (shareholders) need not care who other owners are. This enables shareholders to buy and sell shares without requiring the approval of other owners of the firm. That translates into a substantial reduction in the transaction costs of raising large amounts of capital.

---

[1] Perhaps the best source on the corporation and the rule of limited liability is F. Easterbrook, and D. Fischel, *The Economic Structure of Corporate Law* (Cambridge: Harvard University Press, 1991), chapters 1-2. For a different analysis of the rule of limited liability see R. Ekelund, and R. Tollison *Mercantilism as a Rent-Seeking Society* (College Station: Texas A&M University Press, 1981).

The Myth of Separating Ownership from Control

The owners of the corporation are entitled to capture the residual, to hire and fire cooperating inputs, and to sell those rights in financial markets. The shareholders have the right to choose contractual partners as well as incentives to monitor their performance. Other members of the team are holders of fixed claims.

However, the ownership of many corporations is dispersed among many shareholders. An implication of dispersed shareholding is that individual owners face high transaction costs in exercising their right to hire and fire the firm's management. Combined with management advantages in a proxy fight, the dispersion of shareholding increases the shareholders' costs of hiring, monitoring, and firing their managers.

Critics of the private property economy have assumed that dispersion of shareholding creates a conflict of interest between the shareholders who bear risk and the managers who manage risk. The conflict is supposed to have two consequences. One is withering away of private property rights in the corporate firm, while the other is about the transfer (stealing) of a part of the residual from shareholders to managers. Together, they produced the thesis of the separation of ownership from control.

The first assertion of the separation thesis is that by divorcing ownership from control, the dispersion of stockholding trivializes the meaning of private ownership in corporations. Hard-core socialist scholars from Eastern Europe, such as Branko Horvat from Croatia and Mihailo Markovich from Serbia, have shifted their criticism of private property rights to accommodate new realities. Some decades ago they, like all other devout Marxists, blamed private ownership for transforming humanity into a horde of profit-seeking beasts. Today, they argue that there is no need to encourage the development of private-ownership firms because the dispersion of shareholding has already socialized private property rights in business firms.

The argument is plain wrong. When I purchase a share of Texas Instruments for $100, I tell the management, in effect: "You are better experts at making money than I am. Please take my $100 and do the best you can for me." I voluntarily transfer my control rights to those who, in my judgment, are much better at making money. And I can always choose to take the market value of my investment back. If and when it is less than my initial investment, I bear the costs of my decision.

The second assertion is that by raising the owners' costs of monitoring corporate managers, dispersion of stockholding leads to a transfer (stealing) of wealth from shareholders to managers. The claim is something like this: given their subjective estimate of the shareholders' transaction costs of policing managers' behavior, corporate managers can, within the limits of that estimate, substitute away from the shareholders profits to pursue their own private ends, such as membership in country clubs, plush offices, supporting causes they believe in, and expense accounts. This transfer of wealth is reported as a cost of doing business. Since one dollar in cash offers a greater range of choices than one dollar in nonpecuniary income, the transfer of wealth from shareholders to managers is inefficient.

Empirical observations are consistent with neither of these two criticisms of the corporate firm. How do we explain the fact that millions of individuals continue to invest in common stock? Why do they not choose among many other forms of investment? Why is equity financing not being driven out by investments in fixed claims? Why do we not observe a lower bid price for stocks of corporations with dispersed ownership relative to those firms that have less dispersed ownership? Why do dispersed ownership corporations not have lower rates of growth of shareholders' wealth?

In fact, empirical and theoretical research has not been able to demonstrate the expected inefficiency effects of the dispersion of shareholding. The reason is quite simple. Proponents of the separation thesis have not understood the disciplinary power of competitive markets. Central to this research are the effects of private property rights on transaction costs *via* (1) financial markets, where market valuation of the expected future consequences of current decisions by managers raises their costs of making decisions that are contrary to the interests of shareholders, (2) the competitive markets for managers, and (3) quite importantly, hostile takeovers, leveraged buyouts, and going-private decisions. Michael Jensen, among others, addresses how and why competitive markets, by disciplining corporate managers, have increased the operating efficiency of corporations, their employee productivity, and their shareholder value.[1]

---

[1] See M. Jensen, "Eclipse of the Public Corporation," *Harvard Business Review*, September-October 1989.

THE CODETERMINING FIRM

Codetermination means that employees join shareholders on the board of directors of corporate firms and take an active role in decision making. Germany has been a leader in promoting codetermination in the West. While labor participation in the management of business firms is still a relevant issue in private property, free-market countries in the 1990s, political debate and economic research on codetermination peaked in the late 1970s and early 1980s.

Two major explanations for the introduction of codetermination in Western Europe are the enhancement of industrial policy and the reduction of worker alienation. The concept of industrial policy dates back to the beginning of the industrial age. It has always meant different things to different people in different periods. But the common denominator of industrial policy has never changed: it is a vehicle for labor participation in the management of business firms.

Support for codetermination comes primarily from social engineers, ideologists (mainly neo-Marxists) and European trade unions.

Social engineers see codetermination as a method for bestowing benefits on labor without any detrimental effect to stockholders.[1] They tout the merits of industrial policy without reference to its costs.[2] Yet, a critical effect of codetermination is that nonspecific resources (such as labor) on the board of directors of corporate firms lower the costs of opportunistic behavior.

Marxists support codetermination because it is a step in attenuating the right of ownership. H. Gintis wrote:

> I would argue that in this historical period [capitalism] only an expansion of the degree of democratic and participatory control that individuals have over their lives is compatible with full personal development, rewarding social activity, the

---

[1] E. Batstone, "Industrial Democracy and Worker Representation at Board Level: A Review of the European Experience," *Industrial Democracy Committee Research Report* (London: Her Majesty's Stationery Office, 1976).

[2] For example, Robert Reich's much quoted <u>The Next American Frontier</u> has little to offer in terms of a cost-benefit analysis of industrial policy.

elimination of class, racial, and sexual antagonism, and material equality. The contribution of political democracy to this end is vitiated by the totalitarian organization of production. Only democracy and participation in production-- the replacement of the capitalist class by the working class as the architects of production, and the accountability of managers and technicians to the will of workers--is compatible with equality and full individual development.[1]

European labor leaders are using codetermination as a vehicle for their own economic gains (i.e., by appointing themselves to boards of directors). The extent to which European workers themselves support codetermination is not clear. In 1976, codetermination was defeated in Switzerland, the only country in which the issue has been put to a vote.

American labor unions have refused to embrace codetermination. The president of the Machinists Union said: "We have no interest in replacing free enterprise with a Utopian system.... And we believe workers can receive a better share of free enterprise at the bargaining table than in board rooms."[2] Whatever their motives might have been, American labor leaders saved the country from political pressures to implement contractual agreements that wouldn't emerge spontaneously.

The History of Codetermination in Germany

Codetermination in Germany derives its support from the philosophical origins of industrial democracy. As early as 1835, Robert Von Mohl, Wilhelm Roscher and Bruno Hildebrand, all university professors, proposed to create "workers' committees" in business firms. They felt that capitalism had failed to emphasize moral issues. Their proposal was limited to giving labor the right of hearing. The emphasis was on moral appeals to conscience rather than on legal changes.

In 1848 the first elected German parliament met in Frankfurt. Among other issues, the parliament intended to pass legislation that

---

[1] H. Gintis, "Welfare Economics and Individual development: A Reply to Talcott Persons," *Quarterly Journal of Economics* 89 (May 1975), pp. 301-2.

[2] J. Ellenberger, "The Realities of Codetermination," *AFL-CIO Federationist*, October 1977.

was called Reichgewerbeordnung. This was the first legislative effort in Germany to create representation of workers in business firms.

The law did not pass but an interesting development occurred in subsequent years. Many provisions of this act were voluntarily implemented by a number of firms. The workers and the owners of business firms found it in their self-interest to work out mutually beneficial contractual agreements without resort to the authority of the state (other than to enforce voluntary agreements). The point is that parties to a contract can identify opportunities for exchange, determine their own trade-offs, and negotiate terms of exchange at a lower cost than that at which a third party could possibly do it for them. While law applies equally to all firms, voluntary contracts allow an owner and that owner's workers to identify and exploit opportunities specific to that firm.

This voluntary emergence of contractual agreements within business firms was eventually arrested by the state. Worker committee laws were enacted in Bavaria in 1900 and in Prussia in 1905. These laws began a process of exogenous changes in the employer-employee relationship. Instead of spontaneous development of contractual agreements that could vary from one firm to another in accordance with their own specific problems, the state began to impose a uniform set of rules on all business firms.

In 1920, a works council law was enacted, giving workers the right of hearing in social and personnel questions. In 1922 came another law, according to which one or two employees must be seated on supervisory councils (the equivalent of boards of directors) of business firms. This was the first law on codetermination in Germany. The development that had begun in 1848 had eventually led the country to labor participation in the management of business firms.

In 1946, the military government passed the so-called Act 22, reestablishing works councils. In 1951, came the Montan Act on the "Codetermination of Employees on the Supervisory Councils of Enterprises in the Coal Mining, Iron and Steel Producing Industries" and the stage was set for the current phase in the development of codetermination in Germany. The Montan Act of 1951 covers all firms in the mining and the iron and steel industries that employ at least 1,000 workers. The supervisory council (i.e., the board of directors) of a firm in the Montan industry consists of eleven elected members. Stockholders elect five, employees elect five, and the eleventh member is jointly elected by all supervisory board members.

The Works Constitution Acts of 1952 and 1972 stipulate employees' rights at three different levels of the firm. On the personal level each employee is granted the right of information, hearing, and discussion of issues such as working conditions, hiring, firing, and layoffs. At the plant level, the legislation mandates formation of works councils. These are elected by the employees and vary in size. In general, their function is to act as social agents for the employees in their respective plants. On the decision-making level of the firm, the Works Constitution Acts stipulate that in firms employing more than 500 people, one-third of the members of the supervisory council must be labor representatives.

The Codetermination Act of 1976 applies to all business firms that have more than 2,000 employees. The supervisory council (i.e., the board of directors) for such firms has twelve members, Of which six are representatives of the shareholders and six are representatives of the employees. At least three members representing employees are appointed by labor unions. The chairman of the supervisory council is elected by the shareholders and holds the deciding vote in case of a deadlock.

Empirical evidence is not consistent with the claim that codetermination bestows benefits on workers without any detrimental effects to stockholders. After the passage of the Montan Act in 1951, many business firms tried to escape the parity representation on the supervisory board through mergers, reorganizations, and other structural changes. Those adjustments made them subject only to the one-third employee representative requirement of the Works Constitution Act. In the parliament, in the courts, and through direct pressures on individual firms, German trade unions fought those attempts by business firms to avoid codetermination. The same trend continued after the enactment of the Codetermination Act of 1976. In that year, the Act applied to about 650 firms. In the early 1980s codetermination covered only about 480 firms. About 120 firms had reduced their labor force below the 2,000 limit, while about 50 firms had changed their corporate charters. Assuming that both the size and contractual forms of those 170 firms reflected efficient decisions, the post-1976 adjustments are a social cost of codetermination.

Codetermination, Transaction Costs, and Incentives

There is no law in the United States or Germany or anywhere else in the West that says that there shall be no codetermination. We observe a large number of different types of firms in the West. All these firms have emerged through voluntary contractual negotiations and have survived competition from other types of firms. Why then should Germany (and some other Western European countries) need laws on codetermination? Why has codetermination not emerged voluntarily like the other types of business firms? Indeed, there are cases in which codetermination has emerged voluntarily, but it has not happened on any significant scale. Some quasi-codetermination efforts by employees to buy ownership rights in their enterprises (e.g., United Airlines in 1994) seem limited to declining firms and could be a preferred method of accepting wage cuts.

Those efforts, as long as they have to prove themselves in competitive markets, are not at issue. The issue is the law mandating codetermination and protecting it from competition. The fact that the German government had to mandate the codetermining firm and protect it from competition by other types of firms is the best evidence of its inefficiency. Jensen and Meckling wrote:

> Indeed, labor can start, and in rare cases has started firms of its own. Moreover, firms are free to write any kind of contracts they wish with their employees. If they choose to, they can offer no-dismissal no lay-off contracts (tenure at universities). If they choose to, they can establish worker councils and agree not to change production methods without worker approval. Moreover, employers would establish such practices if the benefits exceeded the costs. Furthermore, if laborers value the security and "self-realization" which such participatory arrangements afford them at more than their costs to the employer, they are in a position to offer voluntary changes which it will pay the employer to take. ...*Since those arrangements are [rarely] observed, we infer that workers do not value the security, management participation, etc. at more than the cost of providing them* [emphasis mine].[1]

---

[1] M. Jensen, and W. Meckling, "Rights and Production Functions: An Application to Labor-Managed Firms and Codetermination," pp. 472-3.

German experience with codetermination reveals some problems. For instance, the election procedure takes up to one year at a cost of millions of marks for direct expenses and loss of working hours. Another cost is that the supervisory council consists of two groups: those representing shareholders and those representing employees. The result is that prior to the official meetings of the board, separate sessions are held by those two groups to work out their respective positions on important issues facing the board. Thus, discussions in the board room are not free exchanges of thoughts, ideas and judgments but a sort of bargaining between the two sides. A case in point was the decision by Volkswagen to open a plant in the United States. The decision was delayed for over two years by the employees' representatives on the board. There is also the question of a conflict of interests. Management is supposed to give the board full information about the firm, and members of the board are to treat information as confidential. However, those who represent workers feel that their obligation to employees supersedes any other obligation.[1]

In general, codetermination changes the prevailing relationships among shareholders, managers, employees, and labor unions. Consequently, it affects decision-making powers, appropriability of rewards, and the relationship between risk taking and bearing of costs in firms. The laws, then, change the way the game is played. The relevant issue is to look into the effects of codetermination on the allocation and use of resources.

Whatever the facade of words, terms such as "industrial democracy" and "labor participation" are code words for wealth transfers. For involuntary codetermination restricts individuals' freedom to negotiate the most beneficial organizational forms. Codetermination shifts the responsibility for decisions to members of the team whose assets are not firm-specific. If the shareholders make an investment decision that is successful, the gains are shared with labor. If, on the other hand, the investment decision is not successful, shareholders alone bear the losses. Codetermination thus violates the risk-reward relationship which, in turn, must raise the cost of equity capital.

---

[1] M. Paul, "Germany's Requiring of Workers on Boards Causes Many Problems," *Wall Street Journal*, December 10, 1979, p. 1.

Codetermination affects incentives to seek the best use for resources. Given the workers' time horizon, which is limited to their expected employment by the firm, the labor-participatory firm has incentives to choose investment alternatives that shift incomes forward and postpone costs. For example, consider two investment alternatives of equal cost. The expected present value of one alternative is $1,000 while the other yields only $750 at a going rate of interest. However, if the returns from the first alternative are expected over a period of 20 years and those of the second over only 5 years, workers have incentives to push management in the direction of choosing the less profitable one. Even in the absence of profit sharing, wage negotiations and subjective perceptions of job security over their time horizon would provide workers with incentives to prefer business decisions that promise larger annual earnings over a limited time period to those policies that maximize the firm's present value.

In a major study on the consequences of codetermination, G. Benelli, C. Loderer and T. Lys[1] found that the nature of contractual relations in the codetermining firm creates following expected tendencies:

1. Employees will favor equity financing for its residual claim nature: debt competes with the financial claims of labor contracts. Therefore, codetermination should lead to a reduction in leverage.

2. Since other fixed financial claims on the firm's cash flows have a negative effect on their wealth, workers will try to limit the growth of the firm's labor force by favoring the adoption of capital-intensive production processes.

3. In choosing among investment opportunities, employees may favor negative net present value projects, as long as those projects decrease the variance of the firm's value sufficiently.

Codetermination: Conflict or Cooperation

Proponents of industrial policy assert that labor participation in the management of business firms would replace conflict with cooperation. They envision an agreement on ends that is impossible to achieve. In the process, proponents of industrial policy fail to consider the

---

[1] G. Benelli, C. Loderer, and T. Lys, "Labor Participation in Corporate Policy Making Decisions: West Germany's Experience with Codetermination," *Journal of Business* 60 (1987).

consequences of contractual agreements that weaken the right of ownership. The right of ownership transfers the guidance of production from specific individuals with limited knowledge, such as regulators, planners and bureaucrats, to the competitive process in which the knowledge of all is used to generate an outcome that no group of individuals could achieve or even foresee.

The fact that codetermination has to be mandated by the government and protected from competition is the best evidence of its inefficiency. If labor participation has positive effects on the firm's productivity, why don't we observe the codetermining firm? Why don't shareholders negotiate with employees a contract that would make both groups better off? If labor participation has to be mandated by law, how can we assert that it is a superior method for organizing production? What are the effects on transaction costs and incentives of giving decision-making powers to nonspecific resources?

SUGGESTED READING

A. Alchian and S. Woodward, "Reflections on the Theory of the Firm," *Journal of Institutional and Theoretical Economics* 143 (1987).

F. Easterbrook, and D. Fischel, *The Economic Structure of Corporate Law* (Cambridge: Harvard University Press, 1991).

S. Pejovich (ed.), *The Codetermination Movement in the West* (Lexington: D.C. Heath and Company, 1978).

Chapter 14

SOCIALISM: THE LABOR-MANAGED FIRM

The labor-managed firm is a socialist version of codetermination: labor participation without private property rights. Like the codetermining firm, the labor-managed firm has failed to emerge spontaneously on a significant scale. It has also failed to perform successfully whenever and wherever imposed by fiat. An implication is that the value of labor participation to the employees of business firms is less than the costs to their contractual partners of providing it. Simply put, the labor-managed firm is inefficient and has failed to pass the market test..

Yet, J. Dreze, E. Meade, J. Svejnar and J. Vanek, among others, have been asserting that the labor-managed firm is or could be an efficient method of organizing production. Accordingly, they have to explain its observed failures and justify using the strong hand of the state to impose it in society. For example, J. Prasnikar and J. Svejnar explained the failure of the labor-managed firm in the former Yugoslavia (the only country that has tried this type of firm on a large scale and over a long period) as follows:

> The strong influence of the League of Communists, the communist oriented trade unions and the various government authorities suggests that one ought to examine seriously the extent to which the behavior of Yugoslav firms resembles that of a proto-typical socialist enterprise rather than that of a labor-managed firm.[1]

The argument that the party's political monopoly and the size of the bureaucracy are to be blamed for the failure of the labor-managed firm in Yugoslavia ignores transaction costs that are specific to this type of organization: the involuntary labor-managed firm needs political

---

[1] J. Prasnikar and J. Svejnar, "Workers' Participation in Management vs. Social Ownership and Government Policies," Working Paper No. 264, Department of Economics, University of Pittsburgh, 1990, p.5

monopoly and the bureaucracy to protect it from competition with other types of teamwork.

The idea of the labor-participatory firm is, however, far from dead. It offers too many opportunities for social engineering and satisfies too many ideological preferences to be discarded on account of its poor showing. Some current proposals for privatizing state firms in Russia, Serbia, Slovakia, Slovenia and Poland contain strong elements of labor participation in management.

Property Rights in the Labor-Managed Firm

Like all other types of enterprises, labor-managed firms differ from each other in terms of internal agreements among members of the team as well as internal codes of behavior. Economic analysis must then begin with the basic bundle of property rights that sets the labor-managed firm apart from other types of business enterprises, determine the consequences of that bundle of rights on transaction costs and incentives, and provide the analytical propositions from which refutable implications can be deduced.

1. *The employees govern the firm.* While the structure of governance might differ from one firm to another, the decision-making structure of the firm can be expected to take into consideration the preferences of the median worker.

2. *Employees have claims on the firm's cash flows.* This right says that the employees of the labor-managed firm are responsible for all the financial and legal obligations of the firm as well as for the allocation of the residual to the wage fund, investments, and any other purpose not explicitly forbidden by law.

3. *The employees' rights to govern the firm and their claims on the firm's cash flows are not transferable.* Transferability of those rights would, in effect, allow the employees to sell both rights, and the labor-managed firm would turn into a private-ownership firm. An important implication of the nontransferability of rights specified under (1) and (2) is that the employees cannot diversify their portfolio of assets to satisfy their risk preferences. This creates incentives for a conservative bias in decisions that have future consequences for the firm.

4. *The employees' rights to govern the firm and their claims on the firm's cash flows terminate when they quit the firm.* To extend

an employee's nontradable claims on the firm's cash flow beyond that person's quit date, as some proponents of the labor-managed firm have suggested, would be costly to implement and monitor. It would also impose a rising burden on the firm's future costs of production.

This specific right makes the employees' time horizon a critical variable in decision making by the team. It is likely that growing firms might experience a decline in the time horizon of a median worker. A 45-year-old worker might have a shorter time horizon than a 25-year-old employee. However, the former's time horizon *with the firm* is likely to be longer than that of a younger worker who hopes to move up by moving around.

5. *To preserve the continuity of the labor-managed firm, members of the team can have only* usus fructus *in the firm's capital assets.* Usus fructus is the right to use an asset belonging to someone else or to rent it to others, but not to sell it. In Yugoslavia this right was expanded to include the firm's right to sell its assets provided that it maintained their book value.

Property rights specified under (1)-(5) above create incentives and transaction costs that explain why the labor-managed firm has failed to emerge spontaneously on a significant scale. To make the firm more attractive, some writers have proposed various immunizing stratagems which either ignore transaction costs specific to the labor-managed economy or tend to privatize labor-managed firms, or both[1]. Of course, trying to improve the efficiency of the labor-managed firm by introducing some elements of private property rights (and holding back on the right to buy and sell claims) begs a question: Why not do even more for the employees by giving them full ownership? Then they could diversify their portfolio of assets, choose their own risk, and transfer resources to more optimistic owners.

---

[1] H. Flakierski, *The Economic System and Income Redistribution in Yugoslavia* (Armonk: M.E. Sharpe, 1989).

Incentives and Transaction Costs.

The bundle of property rights in the labor-managed firm creates some specific transaction costs and incentives. Those incentives and transaction costs affect the investment behavior of labor-managed firms.

Given the bundle of rights that defines the labor-managed firm, the employees can acquire capital assets through a state agency, by renting them from others, by issuing debt claims, and by allocating a part of the residual into the firm's investment fund.

Acquiring capital through a state agency has many efficiency problems, which have been explored by the public choice scholars. It takes an act of faith to assume that the state will be willing to relinquish its control over the assets given to enterprises.

The rental option for acquiring capital assets has two major problems. First, a number of intangible productive assets--such as the firm's investment in the distribution system, the design of products, the training of the labor force, and internal "culture"--cannot be rented. Second, the rental of durable productive assets is a costly method of acquiring capital assets. Rental arrangements create high transaction costs for the owner (including the state) to monitor the use of durable assets, reduced incentives for the user to incur the costs of maintaining and guarding those assets properly, and increased incentives for the user to overuse or misuse rented assets.

It appears, then, that the labor-managed firm's main sources of investable funds are the claims of debt owners and its retained earnings. The former are pure financial claims. As for the latter, since the employees have no ownership claims on the firm's assets, they cannot have claims on the moneys they leave with the firm to purchase new assets. The employees only hold nontradable claims on the firm's return from those assets, and even those claims for only as long as they stay with the firm. Analysis has to distinguish between external and internal financing of investments by the labor-managed firm.

External Financing of Investment by the Labor-Managed Firm

Sources of external funds could be state loans, bank loans, interfirm borrowing, state grants, and perhaps some other moneys. This section concentrates on the effects of bank credit. Other external sources of funds are subject to similar incentives. The relevant issues for analysis of external financing of investment by the labor-managed firm are the employees benefits and costs.

Employees' Benefits from Investments Financed by Bank Loans

The employees of the labor-managed firm have nontransferable claims on the stream of annual returns (B) from any specific investment (I) made by their firm. This property right creates incentives for the employees to transfer the firm's cash flows from the future to the present. The employees can run down inventories, fail to replace capital assets, underinvest in the maintenance of capital goods, vote themselves large pensions with no funding provisions, grant themselves large severance payments, sell long-term bonds with no sinking-fund provisions, and so on.

To alleviate the effects of those incentives, the government has to invest resources in creating, maintaining, and enforcing a number of constraints on the property and contracting rights of the employees. Examples are the depreciation rules for capital assets, the rules for maintaining and repairing physical assets, the rules for severance payments, and so on. An important consequence of these constraints is that they require a costly bureaucracy (high transaction costs) specific to the labor-managed firm.

Implications of the employees' nontradable claims on the firm's cash flows are twofold. First, the employees do not view projects of equivalent present value as being equal--those projects with returns that occur more quickly are preferred to those with even flows, and the latter are preferred to investments with yields bunched in later periods. Second, the absence of financial markets means that the rate of interest does not express the present prices of capital goods relative to their current costs of production; it merely measures a cost of investment.

An employee's benefits from any specific investment (I) are limited to the annual returns (B) from that investment over the employee's expected stay with the firm (t).[1] The time horizon of the median member of the collective or whatever the decision-making

---

[1] The employee's benefits could also be expressed in terms of their present values. We focus on annual returns and costs. It is a simpler approach that has no effect on our results.

group happens to be is then a critical factor in choosing investment projects in the labor-managed firm. In comparison, the time horizon of an investor in the private property, free-market economy is irrelevant because the flow of benefits over the productive life of the assets is available to that worker in one lump sum.

Employees' Costs from Investments Financed by Bank Loans

The employees' costs for any specific investment (I) financed by bank credit are the series of payments (C) to the bank over the time horizon (t). Given the rate of interest, the firm's annual payments depend on the length of time over which the loan has to be repaid (n). The length of the bank loan is a *negotiable* item in the contract between the borrower and the lender. It is thus important to identify the borrower's and the lender's incentives with respect to (n).

Suppose the labor-managed firm secures an investment loan that has to be paid back over a period of time (n). If the time horizon of the firm's employees (t) were equal to or greater than the length of that loan (n), the current group of workers would bear the entire cost of the investment (I). However, if the employees' time horizon fell short of the length of loan, part of the total cost of the investment (I) would be shifted to the next generation of workers in the same firm.

The employees of the labor-managed firm, then, have incentives to seek investment loans with as lengthy a repayment schedule as the banks are willing to go along with. Employees have incentives to negotiate agreements to pay only interest on investment loans over the current employees' time horizon.

The employees' annual costs of any specific investment (I) financed by bank credit are then

$$C = I \frac{i(1+i)^n}{(1+i)^n - 1}$$

where (n) is the length of bank loan.

The Choice of Investment Projects by Labor-Managed Firms

The employees' benefits from an investment project are the expected returns (B) over their time horizon. Employees' costs from that same investment are the annual payments to the bank (C) over their time horizon. The investment decision of the labor-managed firm depends on the relationship between these two flows. To simplify discussion, we assume that both flows are uniform over the employees' time horizon. Uneven flows would generate different solutions but they would not change incentives. Since the length of loan (n) is determined *contractually* between the lender and the borrower of investment funds, it is possible to adjust (n) so that

$$B = I \frac{i(1+i)^n}{(1+i)^n - 1}$$

This equality shows the minimum time (n*) required to make a specific investment project acceptable to the employees of the labor-managed firm. The investment decision of the firm, then, depends on the ability of its manager to negotiate a loan that, at the minimum, has to be repaid over a period of time that makes the flow of returns from an investment equal to its production costs times the flow of income over (n*) years from $1 now.

Hence, the length of bank credit (n) is a critical variable in the labor-managed firm's choice of investments.

This result is contrary to the views of Meade, Vanek, and other proponents of the labor-managed firm, who argue that the market rate of interest is a critical variable that assures the system of the efficiency of externally financed investments.[1] The difference between the two sets of results arises from these scholars' failure to adjust their models for transaction costs and incentives specific to the labor-managed firm. Emphasizing the importance of incentives and transaction costs, Jensen and Meckling wrote: "Ignoring the agency costs of alternative contractual forms in comparing two systems where the only difference

---

[1] J. Meade, "The Labor-Managed Firm in Conditions of Imperfect Competition," *Economic Journal* 84 (1974); J. Vanek, *The Labor-Managed Economy* (Ithaca: Cornell University Press, 1977).

between the two is the contractual form allowed is unlikely to shed light on the major issues. But Dreze, as well as most other writings on the topic, does exactly this."[1]

The Effects of Changes in the Length of Bank Credit

Suppose that the employees of a labor-managed firm are considering an asset that costs $1,000,000, has a productive life of 15 years, and promises to yield $118,326 per year over a period of 15 years. At the market rate of interest of 10 percent, the present value of that asset is $900,000, and the investment is clearly inefficient. However, suppose that the manager of the firm is able to borrow $1,000,000 from the bank on a 20-year loan at 10 percent. A private-ownership firm would still turn the project down, but the labor-managed firm would not. The employees' annual payments to the bank would be $117,460 per year, while their annual benefits are $118,326. As long as the employees' time horizon is 15 years or less, they would have $866 every year to divide among themselves. Thus they have incentives to make an inefficient investment. The cost shifted to the next generation of workers, including current employees whose time horizon exceeds 15 years, is $117,460 per year over the last five years of the contract.

If the length of the loan is 19.57 years, the firm's *annual* payments (C) to the bank would be equal to *annual* returns (B) from that investment. However, a 20-year loan gives the employees an additional $866 per year over their time horizon with the firm.

An implication is that the manager of the firm has incentives to offer some people at the bank the equivalent of up to $866 per year in cash or specific nonpecuniary goods (free travel, a new TV, etc.) in exchange for a 20-year loan at the market rate of interest.

And the manager would offer even better rewards for longer loans. Table 14-1 shows how changes in the length of the loan increase the amount of money the manager can offer in exchange for a lengthy contract.

Suppose the time horizon of the team is 10 years, and the firm has three investment projects under consideration. The productive life of each project and their respective annual streams of benefits per $1

---

[1] M. Jensen and W. Meckling, "Rights and Production Functions: An Application to Labor-Managed Firms and Codetermination," p. 480.

are shown in Table 14-2, columns 1 and 2. Column 3 shows the minimum length of bank loan (n*) that makes the annual flow of benefits equal to the employees' annual cost of those investments. At a 10 percent rate of interest, a private-ownership firm would clearly turn down all three projects because the present value of each project at the 10 percent rate of interest is 90 cents. However, if the manager of the firm were able to negotiate loans in excess of the critical rate of (n*) years, the employees would find all three investments acceptable.

Table 14-1. The Length of Loan and Rewards

Loan in years	Benefits (B) in $$	Costs (C) in $$	Benefits minus Costs
19.56	118,326	118,326	-0-
20	118,326	117,460	866
21	118,326	115,624	2,702
22	118,326	114,005	4,321
23	118,326	112,572	5,754
24	118,326	111,300	7,026
25	118,326	110,168	8,158

Table 14-2. Property Rights and the Investment Decision

Life of Asset in years	Benefit (B) in $$	Minimum Length of Loan (n*)
10	.146	12.12
15	.118	19.73
20	.106	30.13

A consequence of incentives and transaction costs specific to the labor-managed firm is that *the minimum length of bank credit n* (or of any other financial claim) in relation to the employees' time horizon becomes the critical variable for the choice of investments.*

The employees of the labor-managed firm have incentives to negotiate bank loans in excess of their time horizon. One way of arguing for a longer repayment schedule is to exaggerate the life expectancy of assets to be purchased by loans, not a difficult task given the absence of financial markets or asymmetrical information favoring the borrower or both. And when the length of bank credit exceeds the employees' time horizon, the labor-managed firm has incentives to undertake inefficient investment projects such as those in Table 14-2.[1]

On the other hand, the absence of tradable claims in financial markets must increase the lender's information costs about both the productivity and the life expectancy of assets to be financed by loans, relative to such information costs in private property, free-market economies. The issue is then whether the lender has incentives to incur those costs in order to negotiate contracts that would equalize the length of loans with the life of assets to be purchased with those loans.[2] There are many possible types of lending institutions, such as private-ownership banks,[3] labor-managed banks,[4] various financial institutions, government agencies, and even the so-called super bank.[5]

The fact that the labor-managed firm has not emerged on a significant scale in private property, free-market economies is evidence that the market for business organizations considers *the length of bank credit to be greater than the employees' time horizon, and the lender's incentives and transaction costs insufficient to offset the employees' incentives to seek loans in excess of their time horizon.*

---

[1] When the employees' time horizon is greater than the productive life of assets, the relationship between (t) and (n) still determines whether an inefficient investment is chosen.

[2] Even if that were the case, such contracts would not eliminate inefficient investments. For that to happen, the time horizon of the employees of the labor-managed firm has to be longer than the expected life of assets.

[3] Given the absence of tradable claims in financial markets, it is difficult to envision the flow of private funds into labor-managed firms.

[4] Labor-managed banks have yet to happen voluntarily. And if they did emerge spontaneously, the employees' incentives would be for safe loans at the market rate of interest over their time horizon plus whatever "profit-sharing" agreements with the borrower could bring in exchange for longer repayment schedules.

[5] The super bank was invented by Vanek as a government agency which was to make the labor-managed economy efficient by allocating resources to competing firms at prices (interest rates) that clear the market. Like Lange some decades ago, Vanek argued the case for socialism by ignoring the effects of institutions on incentives and transaction costs, a typical case of mechanical application of neoclassical economics to an alien environment. What are the applicant's incentives to tell the truth about the expected life of its capital goods? What are the incentives of the super bank employees? Do they have incentives to find out the expected life of assets the bank is supposed to finance? What is the cost to the bank's superior of making sure that investment funds are allocated at market-clearing prices? What are the costs of preventing super bank employees from approving longer loans and sharing the resulting profits with the borrower?

Internal Financing of Investment by the Labor-Managed Firm.

The employees' nontradable claims on the firm's cash flows create two wealth-increasing options for them. The employees can take the firm's residual out as wages and invest in assets such as savings accounts they would own. The employees can also leave a part of the residual with the firm (i.e., take less out as current wages) for investment in new capital assets in which they would hold nontradable claims contingent on employment by the firm.[1]

The employees have the right of ownership in savings accounts (or other owned-assets). They can trade those assets, give them away, will them to heirs, or do anything else with them that is not explicitly forbidden by law. On the other hand, the employees have only nontradable claims on the returns from assets held by the firm. They have claims on neither the assets that their sacrifice of current wages made possible nor the year-to-year returns from those assets once they leave the firm. The employees' cost of any specific investment (I) financed from the firm's residual is the sum total on annuities (y) they could have received over the period (t) by taking the amount equal to (I) out as income and saving their respective shares at the going rate of interest (i). Such an annuity for one dollar is

$$y = \frac{i(1+i)^t}{(1+i)^t - 1}$$

The employees' benefits from the same investment (I) financed from the firm's residual is the flow of returns (B) over their time horizon (t). For the employees to be indifferent between internally financed investments and their own individual savings, the former must earn the rate of return (r*) equal to (y); that is, the required rate of return (r*) must be equal to the annuity from one dollar at the rate (i) over the

---

[1] Implications of those differences are examined in detail in S. Pejovich, "The Firm, Monetary Policy and Property Rights," *Western Economic Journal* 7 (1969), M. Jensen and W. Meckling, "Rights and Production Functions: An Application to Labor-Managed Firms and Codetermination," and a series of papers by Eirik Furubotn and Svetozar Pejovich.

employees' time horizon (t).[1] The rate of return (r*) is then the rate of interest (i) <u>adjusted</u> for the incentive effects of property rights in the labor-managed firm:

$$r^* = \frac{i(1+i)^t}{(1+i)^t - 1}$$

The rate of return that would make the employees indifferent between investments that are internally financed and their own private investments could be easily calculated. At a 10 percent interest rate and time horizons of 5, 10 and 15 years, (r*) is 26 percent, 16 percent and 13 percent respectively. Also, as in the case of externally financed investments, equivalent-return projects which pay off quickly would be favored relative to those for which payoffs occur further in the future. Once again, incentives and transaction costs apply that are specific to the prevailing property rights in the labor-managed firm.[2]

SUGGESTED READINGS

D. Prychitko and J. Vanek, *Producer Cooperatives and Labor-Managed Systems* (Cheltenham: Edward Elgar, 1996)

---

[1] This assumes that the two investments are alike with respect to risk level and liquidity. Adding a more detailed assessment of risk and liquidity could only favor private savings.

[2] It is important to understand that the purpose of analysis here is not to demonstrate the inefficiency of the labor-managed firm. The market for the types of business firms has done that. The analysis is aimed at explaining why the labor-managed firm is inefficient. Also, the analysis applies only to labor-managed firms imposed by fiat and protected from competition by other firms.

Chapter 15

PROPERTY RIGHTS, BUSINESS FIRMS, AND INNOVATION

Innovation means doing something that has not been done before. It could be the production of a new good, the opening up of a new market, the discovery of a new source of supply, the development of a new method of production, or changes in the rules of the game that reduce transaction costs. Whichever the case, by injecting a novelty into the flow of economic life, innovation offers the community a new choice. Thus innovation is the engine of economic progress.

Most innovations that affect the economy are technological. Technology, broadly defined, embodies the prevailing knowledge. The growth of knowledge then creates new technological possibilities. Since both the growth and the direction of new knowledge are unpredictable, the flow of innovations is also unpredictable and their impact on the economy uncertain. The innovator translates new technological possibilities into new choices. That is, innovation is a consequence of the individual's perceptions about the applicability of technology, willingness to accept the risk and uncertainty associated with doing something new, and ability to see the innovation through. Accordingly, the innovator must possess traits such as ingenuity, stubbornness, perseverance, and imagination. Boards of directors, governments, agencies, organizations and other groups cannot innovate. A member of one of those groups has to perceive an opportunity to innovate and sell it to colleagues. Potential innovators are virtually impossible to identify *ex ante*, and innovation is not an activity we can plan for. We cannot decide to have two innovations per month.

Innovation is an addition to the community's set of opportunity choices. The implementation of a novelty requires that resources be withdrawn from other uses. By implication, innovation is a trade-off between (1) the value of the output which resources used by the innovator were producing before and (2) the use of those resources to make an addition to the community's set of choices. Voluntary acceptance of an innovation means that the community is better off. Otherwise, innovation would have failed.

The innovator is then a true leader of the system, while the rest of the community gets to judge the innovator's entrepreneurial decisions. An implication is that there is no way to tell whether innovations that are not voluntarily accepted by interacting individuals benefit the community. State authorities have the power to impose and enforce policies regarding innovation. Such policies, as Karl Brunner noted, can have unintended adverse consequences:

> The tragically crippled and deformed babies resulting from the use of thalidomide by pregnant women influences....regulatory policies. The measures implemented raised the costs of development for new products by a large factor... Innovation declined by a sharp margin and the appearance of new drugs sharply contracted....A policy addressed to minimize the probability of bad products maximized at the same time the probability of NOT having useful drugs.[1]

One might say that innovation unfolds the meaning of economic development as the expansion of choices voluntarily accepted by the community. Economic development is neither about more of the same nor about new choices imposed on the community from without.

PROPERTY RIGHTS AND THE FLOW OF INNOVATION

If innovation cannot be planned for and if innovators cannot be identified in advance, economic development cannot be charted either. The best economic analysis can do is to identify the factors that affect the flow of innovation in the community and the circumstances upon which those factors depend. Research and empirical studies have shown that property rights structures are one such factor. Douglass North has received a Nobel prize for demonstrating a strong link between different types of property rights and economic development. This chapter analyzes the effect of three types of property rights in business firms (discussed in chapters eleven and twelve) on the flow of

---

[1] K. Brunner, "The Limits of Economic Policy," in *Socialism: Institutional, Philosophical and Economic Issues*, in S. Pejovich, ed. (Dordrecht: Kluwer Academic Publishers, 1987), pp. 41-42.

innovation. Analysis is divided into four sections: freedom to innovate, incentives to innovate, the power to innovate, and the integration of innovation into the economy.

Freedom to Innovate

Potential innovators do not emerge from a specific social class. They come from all social groups. Thus the larger the number of people who have the freedom to innovate, the higher the probability of increasing the flow of innovation.

In a private property economy, everyone has the right to acquire resources and use them to pursue any lawful activity, including innovation. However, private property rights are often attenuated in free societies. Codetermination laws in Germany raise the cost of equity capital, license requirements reduce the number of people who can pursue specific activities, monopoly privileges including foreign trade restrictions limit one's right to choose how to use one's own resources, the Food and Drug Administration delays and perhaps discourages some innovators. While it is wrong to argue that no restriction of private property rights yields positive benefits, the attenuation of private property has to affect the flow of innovation by interfering with the freedom to innovate.

In a centrally planned economy, entry into decision making is through membership in the ruling elite, which is a self-perpetuating group joined primarily through personal connections, and from which one departs through death or political disgrace. Individuals (including members of the ruling elite) have no right to acquire productive resources. Members of the ruling elite, managers of enterprises, and all other individuals who perceive an opportunity for an innovation must sell the idea to their colleagues or superiors, who in turn have to sell it to their superiors, and so on. The right to acquire and use resources in a centrally planned economy is then effectively limited to the ruling elite.

In a labor-managed economy, the pool of those who have the right to acquire and use resources is restricted to the working collective. The term "working collective" is important here. Only a working collective, either directly or through its governing board, can decide to carry out innovations. An employee who perceives an opportunity to innovate must sell the idea to the workers' council--a group of people with limited business experience, diverse attitudes toward risk, inadequate understanding of production techniques and market processes, and short time horizons.

Incentives to Innovate

A successful innovation yields benefits in excess of what the bundle of resources used by the innovator was earning before. However, innovation is a nonroutine activity, and the level of risk associated with it is not known. The innovator has to choose, in effect, between investing a bundle of resources in a project for which the outcome is unpredictable, or in one of the routine activities for which the risk is known. This is the cost of innovation. The innovator's decision whether to accept the cost of innovation must depend on the prevailing incentives.

In a private property economy, the innovator can appropriate the present value of the expected benefits from a successful innovation either in one lump sum (by selling it to another person) or as a stream of payments. A private property, free-market economy provides incentives to innovate even for those who do not own resources. For example, the manager of a privately owned firm benefits from a successful innovation through the market for managers, in which the current profitability of the enterprise affects his earnings *via* competing offers by other firms.

The gains from a successful innovation are only temporary. In a private property, free-market economy, the gains attract duplications and imitations. That is, the choice between routine investments and innovation has to be influenced by the expected length of the imitation gap--the purpose of copyrights, patents, etc., is to extend this lag in order to encourage the innovator. In fact, if all potential rivals were able to imitate successful innovations quickly, incentives to innovate would be seriously impaired. Transaction costs are, however, positive and high. The gap between the novelty and the routine use of resources, which is the source of the innovator's gain, endures because it takes time, effort, and resources for potential rivals to learn, evaluate, and implement new technology.

The prevailing property rights in a labor-managed economy (i.e., the absence of transferable claims on the returns from capital goods) have two consequences that tend to dampen the collective's incentives to innovate. First, the absence of the right to capitalize the expected future benefits into their present market price means that the working collective cannot appropriate the expected benefits of a successful innovation in one lump sum. Relative to a free-market, private property economy, the innovator has fewer options for appropriating the benefits of a successful innovation. Second, since the collective can capture the benefits only as they occur, its members (e.g., those who expect to retire soon or change jobs) must have a bias against innovations that are expected, if successful, to yield benefits over a long period of time.

In a planned economy, any individual (e.g., the manager of a firm) is free to propose an innovation to a superior. However, there is a world of difference between the right to make suggestions and the right to do things. For at least two reasons, a member of the ruling elite has reduced incentives to try to push an innovation through the channels. First, decisions to innovate are not made by individuals. They are reviewed and debated by layers of various committees, the members of which are likely to prefer not to rock the boat. Second, the private costs of pushing a specific innovation through the channels are substantial. If the innovation is a success, the innovator will share the benefits with colleagues and superiors. If it is a failure, colleagues and superiors will blame the innovator.

Socialist states did (and still do) attempt to alleviate the absence of incentives to innovate via various awards such as Lenin prizes, Tito's prizes, monetary bonuses, free vacations and larger apartments. But those attempts avoided granting more property rights to potential innovators. Thus, they were not strong enough to offset the effects of the absence of credible and stable incentive structures on the flow of innovation. Leszek Balcerowicz, the first Minister of Finance in post-communist Poland, argued that the then prevailing institutional structures in a Soviet-type economy were totally incapable of either producing scientific innovations or imitating technological developments abroad. Balcerowicz's point was that information about Western technological innovations, which the Soviets used to steal at high cost, was generally useless to them.

The Power to Innovate

Freedom to acquire and use resources is not the same thing as actually having the power to get them. In a private property economy, capital markets match the quantity of financial assets demanded with the quantity supplied to reflect contractual agreements on various issues, including risks. The ability to acquire an asset in financial markets depends on the borrower having enough resources to pay for it, and the lender having a bundle of rights in the asset and being willing to transfer these at a price the borrower is willing to pay.

The ability of a privately owned firm to innovate is more likely to be limited by transaction costs arising from its organizational structure and size than by financial markets. The larger the firm and the greater the number of people who have to say "yes" as an innovation unfolds, the more costly it is to carry out the innovation. Moreover, a major issue facing the management of successful firms in a private property economy is how to preserve flexibility, creativity, and adaptability as the company gets bigger and its initial vigor yields to the process of maturing. Pat Haggerty, a founder of Texas Instruments, remarked that the firm's top management spent many months trying to find a way to institutionalize the process of proposing, approving and implementing innovations so that the company could retain its leadership in technology. We can say that private property rights provide an institutional framework within which new firms with humble beginnings, such as Macintosh, can acquire the power to innovate, while such rights give mature firms like Texas Instruments an opportunity to regain their initial vigor.

In a labor-managed economy, the nontransferability of the employees' claims on the firm's cash flows and the fact that those nontransferable claims are also contingent on people's employment with that firm reduce the collective's ability to innovate. As discussed in chapter twelve, the absence of financial markets leaves the labor-managed firm with two major sources of investable funds: retained earnings and bank credit, neither of which is a promising source of funds for innovation.

The ability to innovate in a centrally planned economy is limited to those innovations that are approved by economic planners, and it usually requires a miracle to get the bureaucracy to go along with a risky novelty. A remarkable 1957 book by Vladimir Dudincev, which has not aged with the passage of time, describes the frustration of an engineer in the USSR who has an idea for a technical innovation but is faced with the entrenched bureaucracy, which would rather destroy him than approve a risky venture.[1]

Integration of Innovation into the Economy

A novelty does not necessarily make people better off. It has to be voluntarily accepted *and* integrated into the economy. In a private property economy, competitive markets evaluate the novelty. Freedom of exchange reveals the costs and benefits of the novelty as perceived by interacting individuals. And those costs and benefits, *via* relative prices, tell us whether or not the innovation has enriched the community. By internalizing the gains from a successful innovation, private property rights encourage a greater flow of innovation than do collective or state property rights under socialism.

A greater flow in innovations has two consequences. First, it raises the average income in the community; the assumption being that a larger flow of innovation tends to produce a larger number of successful innovations. Second, a greater flow of innovations increases the mobility of individuals between income classes without any appreciable effect on the distribution of income. Initially, successful innovators earn more money than before. However, the resulting increase in income inequalities is only a temporary phenomenon. Large incomes of successful innovators are eventually whittled away through market competition via lower prices paid by consumers and higher prices of resources used to imitate innovations. For example, the distribution of income in the United States has remained relatively stable over several decades in spite of different growth rates during those years. The income share of the poorest 20 percent of families in the United States was about 4.5 percent of the total national income in 1950 and 4.6 percent in 1990; the income share of the wealthiest 20 percent was 42.7 percent of the total in 1950 and 44.3 percent in 1990.[2]

Integration of innovation in a labor-managed economy has three limitations, all of which can be attributed to the prevailing property rights. First, although a successful innovation creates larger

---

[1] V. Dudincev, *Not By Bread Alone* (New York: E.P. Dutton & Company, 1957).
[2] United States Bureau of Census, "Current Population Report," Series P-60, No. 174, 1993.

profits for the collective implementing it, it is less likely to spread to other firms than would be the case under a capitalist system: the absence of financial markets raises the cost of information to potential rivals. Second, when information about larger profits becomes available, only existing firms enter into competition with the innovating firm. The entry of new firms in a labor-managed economy has to be slow because it requires a group decision to create a new firm. Third, suppose that rival firms have to hire additional workers in order to compete with the innovating firm. Given the prevailing property rights, new workers are new policy makers as well. This means that in order to ensure the security of its common interests, the current collective has incentives to trade off some pecuniary income that could be had by hiring additional workers. Thus, it is only at significant costs that the labor-managed firm provides signals regarding whether the community has or has not accepted an innovation. It means that a labor-managed economy has a predictable tendency to maintain money-income inequalities created by successful innovations.

In a centrally planned economy, the absence of both private property rights and contractual freedom (i.e., competitive prices) makes the costs of knowing whether the community has or has not accepted an innovation staggeringly high. Acceptance of an innovation requires its evaluation in terms of the value that resources used by the innovator would have created if they were employed elsewhere. But the only thing that can be the for an innovation is individuals interacting with other individuals in a free setting.

SUGGESTED READING

L Balcerowicz, "The Soviet-Type Economic System and Innovativeness," Institute for Economic Development, Warsaw, 1988, working paper No. 19.

J. Moore, "Measuring Soviet Economic Growth: Old Problems and New Complications," *Journal of Institutional and Theoretical Economics* 148 (1992).

INDEX

A

Adelstein 10
Albert 125
Alchian.19, 36, 37, 38, 53, 63, 70, 101, 110, 112, 113, 168, 169, 170, 172, 173, 177, ... 178, 180, 194
Allen 110, 112, 113, 170, 172, 173
Anderson 93
Arndt 164

B

Bacon 77
Benelli 193
Boyd 24
Breton 125, 137
Brunner 5, 6, 19, 121, 208
Buchanan 40, 44, 70, 92, 126

C

Calvin 78
Coase 9, 10, 12, 13, 19, 28
Colombatto 123, 151, 156
Comte 77, 84
Crawford 178
Cukierman 55

D

David 37, 38, 77, 88
Davidson 93
Davis 34
Demsetz 14, 15, 67
Descartes 77
Dreze 195, 202
Dudincev 212, 213

E

Ekelund 72, 73, 75, 83, 93, 184
Ellickson 28

F

Ferguson 110

Flakierski ... 197

G

Gintis ... 187, 188

H

Haggard ... 160
Haggerty ... 212
Hayek ... 29, 31, 91, 128
Hebert ... 93
Horvat ... 185
Hume ... 77

J

Jensen ... 53, 169, 170, 174, 179, 180, 186, 191, 201, 202, 205

K

Kant ... 77
Klein ... 178

L

Laidler ... 85
Lal ... 78, 164
Lange ... 177, 204
Lenin ... 30, 139, 211
Libecap ... 34, 35
Locke ... 77
Loderer ... 193
Luther ... 78
Lys ... 193

M

Macey ... 151, 156
Manchester ... 73, 75, 76, 77
Markovich ... 185
Marx ... 27, 30, 84, 85, 86, 87, 88, 89, 90, 139
McAvoy ... 121
McManus ... 172
Meade ... 195, 201
Meckling ... 53, 169, 170, 174, 179, 180, 191, 201, 202, 205
Meltzer ... 55
Mises ... 82, 83, 177
Moore ... 214

N

Niskanen ... 30, 31, 137
North ... 15, 17, 18, 24, 28, 34, 37, 38, 46, 47, 68, 79, 93, 151, 208
Nutter ... 30, 149

O

Olson 132
Ostrom 65
Owen 85

P

Petroni 31
Posner 17, 40, 41, 44
Prasnikar 195
Prychitko 206

R

Reich 187
Ricardo 88
Richerson 24

S

Schumpeter 81
Simon 7, 84
Smith 59, 77, 81, 83
Stigler 43, 92, 122
Svejnar 195
Szakadat 175

T

Tollison 93, 184
Tullock 126

V

Vanek 195, 201, 204, 206
Verdier 131, 158

W

Wallis 17, 18
Weber 77, 78
Williams 39
Winter 14
Woodward 53, 177, 180, 194

International Studies in Economics and Econometrics

1. T. Harder: *Introduction to Mathematical Models in Market and Opinion Research.* With Practical Applications, Computing Procedures, and Estimates of Computing Requirements. Translated from German. 1969 ISBN 90-277-0096-6
2. A.R.G. Heesterman: *Forecasting Models for National Economic Planning.* 2nd rev. and ext. ed. 1972 ISBN 90-277-0224-1
3. A.R.G. Heesterman: *Allocation Models and Their Use in Economic Planning.* 1971 ISBN 90-277-0182-2
4. M. Durdağ: *Some Problems of Development Financing.* A Case Study of the Turkish First Five-Year Plan (1963-1967). 1973
 ISBN 90-277-0267-5
5. J.M. Blin: *Patterns and Configurations in Economic Science.* 1973
 ISBN 90-277-0203-7
6. A.H.Q.M. Merkies: *Selection of Models by Forecasting Intervals.* Translated from Dutch. 1973 ISBN 90-277-0342-6
7. H.C. Bos, M. Sanders and C. Secchi: *Private Foreign Investment in Developing Countries.* A Quantitative Study on the Evaluation of the Macro-Economic Effects. 1974
 ISBN Hb 90-277-0410-4; Pb 90-277-0439-2
8. R. Frisch: *Economic Planning Studies.* A Collection of Essays. Selected, introduced and edited by Frank Long, with a Preface by Jan Tinbergen. 1976 ISBN Hb 90-277-0245-4; Pb 90-277-1194-1
9. K.L. Gupta and M. A. Islam: *Foreign Capital, Savings and Growth.* An International Cross-Section Study. 1983 ISBN 90-277-1449-5
10. C.A. van Bochove: *Imports and Economic Growth.* 1982
 ISBN 90-247-3052-X
11. O. Bjerkholt and E. Offerdal (eds.): *Macroeconomic Prospects for a Small Oil Exporting Country.* 1985 ISBN 90-247-3183-6
12. D. Weiserbs (ed.): *Industrial Investment in Europe.* Economic Theory and Measurement. 1985 ISBN 90-247-3270-0
13. J.-M. Graf von der Schulenburg and G. Skogh (eds.): *Law and Economics & The Economics of Legal Regulation.* 1986
 ISBN 90-247-3377-4
14. S. Pejovich (ed.): *Socialism: Institutional, Philosophical and Economic Issues.* 1987 ISBN 90-247-3487-8
15. R. Heijmans and H. Neudecker (eds.): *The Practice of Econometrics.* Studies on Demand, Forecasting, Money and Income. In Honor of Jan Salomon Cramer. 1987 ISBN 90-247-3502-5
16. A. Steinherr and D. Weiserbs (eds.): *Employment and Growth.* Issues for the 1980s. In Honor of Albert Kervyn de Lettenhove. 1987
 ISBN 90-247-3514-9
17. M.J. Holler (ed.): *The Logic of Multiparty Systems.* 1987
 ISBN 90-247-3515-7

International Studies in Economics and Econometrics

18. J.M. van Brabant: *Regional Price Formation in Eastern Europe.* Theory and Practice of Trade Pricing. 1987   ISBN 90-247-3540-8
   See also below under Volume 23
19. A.M. Wesselman: *The Population-Sample Decomposition Method.* A Distribution-Free Estimation Technique for Minimum Distance Parameters. 1987   ISBN 90-247-3603-X
20. P. Coffey (ed.): *Main Economic Policy Areas of the EEC – Toward 1992.* The Challenge to the Community's Economic Policies when the 'Real' Common Market is Created by the End of 1992. 3rd rev.ed., 1990   ISBN 0-7923-0810-7
21. A. Breton, G. Galeotti, P. Salmon and R. Wintrobe (eds.): *The Competitive State.* Villa Colombella Papers on Competitive Politics. 1991
     ISBN 0-7923-0835-2
22. S. Pejovich: *The Economics of Property Rights.* Towards a Theory of Comparative Systems. 1990   ISBN 0-7923-0878-6
23. J.M. van Brabant: *Remaking Eastern Europe.* On the Political Economy of Transition. 1990   ISBN 0-7923-0955-3
24. J.M. van Brabant: *Privatizing Eastern Europe.* The Role of Markets and Ownership in the Transition. 1992   ISBN 0-7923-1861-7
25. J.M. van Brabant: *Integrating Eastern Europe into the Global Economy.* Convertibility through a Payments Union. 1991
     ISBN 0-7923-1352-6
26. G.W. Kołodko, D. Gotz-Kozierkiewicz and E. Skrzeszewska-Paczek: *Hyperinflation and Stabilization in Postsocialist Economies.* 1992
     ISBN 0-7923-9179-9
27. P. Mihályi: *Socialist Investment Cycles.* Analysis in Retrospect. 1992
     ISBN 0-7923-1973-7
28. A. Breton, G. Galeotti, P. Salmon and R. Wintrobe (eds.): *Preferences and Democracy.* Villa Colombella Papers on Competitive Politics. 1993   ISBN 0-7923-9321-X
29. K.Z. Poznanski (ed.): *Stabilization and Privatization in Poland.* An Economic Evaluation of the Shock Therapy Program. 1993
     ISBN 0-7923-9341-4
30. P. Coffey (ed.): *Main Economic Policy Areas of the EC-After 1992.* 4th Revised Edition. 1993   ISBN 0-7923-2375-0
31. J.M. van Brabant: *Industrial Policy in Eastern Europe.* Governing the Transition. 1993   ISBN 0-7923-2538-9
32. H.J. Blommestein and B. Steunenberg (eds.): *Government and Markets.* Establishing a Democratic Constitutional Order and a Market Economy in Former Socialist Countries. 1994   ISBN 0-7923-3059-5
33. S. Pejovich: *Economic Analysis of Institutions and Systems.* 1995 Revised Edition. 1997   ISBN 0-7923-8031-2

International Studies in Economics and Econometrics

34. R. Holzmann, J. Gács and G. Winckler (eds.): *Output Decline in Eastern Europe.* Unavoidable, External Influence or Homemade? 1995 ISBN 0-7923-3285-7
35. P. Coffey: *Europe – Toward 2001.* 1996
ISBN 0-7923-3891-X; Pb 0-7923-3892-8
36. M. Mejstrik: *The Privatization Process in East Central Europe.* 1996
ISBN 0-7923-4096-5
37. J.M. van Brabant: *Integrating Europe.* The Transition Economies. 1996 ISBN 0-7923-9806-8

KLUWER ACADEMIC PUBLISHERS – DORDRECHT / BOSTON / LONDON